EVENTS
THAT CHANGED THE
WORLD

igloobooks

igloobooks

Published in 2017
by Igloo Books Ltd
Cottage Farm
Sywell
NN6 0BJ
www.igloobooks.com

HUN001 0817
2 4 6 8 10 9 7 5 3
ISBN 978-1-78557-251-7

Cover images: (tl) © DC Stock / Alamy Stock Photo; (tc) © IanDagnall Computing / Alamy Stock Photo;
(tr) © Dennis Hallinan / Alamy Stock Photo; (br) US Air Force Photo / Alamy Stock Photo;
(bc) Popperfoto / Getty Images; (bl) Spencer Platt / Getty Images

Cover designed by Charles Wood-Penn
Edited by Natalie Baker

Written by Carrie Lewis

Printed and manufactured in China

Contents

Introduction

Time is the way that we measure the endless thread of seconds, hours and years that make our lives and our history. Time may appear to stand still or to slip away before we are ready. It may appear to be all the same, or to change so constantly that it is beyond our ability to understand. Some moments in time, however, stand out from all the others either as brilliant gems or as terrible knots along the thread of time. This book is intended to remember and celebrate the most significant moments of the last century, and bring them to life.

The century we have just passed through has been the first that we have been able to witness through film and photography. Many of the events in this book relate to new things that have been seen using technology, for example Hubble seeing new stars with the Hale telescope, and Curiosity sending back pictures from Mars. Changes like these have affected our understanding of the universe beyond recognition. Other achievements in science are also celebrated and explored here such as the discovery of vaccines and the ability to perform heart transplants. These breakthrough moments in medical science have changed life for millions worldwide.

Many events in this book describe the rapid pace of social change seen throughout the Twentieth Century, especially with regard to racial equality. Events such as the Civil Rights March in Washington, Rosa Parks' refusal to get off the bus and the imprisonment of Nelson Mandela remind us that this century has, for some people, been one of oppression and struggle. Through extraordinary courage and perseverance, however, some of this oppression has now been overcome and greater importance is given to human rights in the light of this century's great civil rights pioneers.

Perhaps the greater part of the events listed in this book relate to significant moments of political change, for example through wars and battles, or in the actions of leaders. Some of these events, like the bombing of Hiroshima or the first day of the Somme, make for difficult reading as we reflect on the rights and wrongs, or on the terrible loss of life that can come with the dawn of a single day. Other events, however, such as the signing of the Declaration of Human Rights, show that history can be a great teacher, and that the lessons of these terrible events can be put to good use saving future lives.

Looking back into the past, one end of the thread of time recedes into a grey mist of half-remembered moments, faces and events. Who knows where the other end will lead? The most recent events in this book reveal a present time that is full of optimism and invention. Whether it is a brilliant gem or a terrible knot in the thread of time, enjoy each moment as it is brought to life here and imagine what wonders we may have to ponder at the end of the century that is just beginning.

1900–1920

1905 Einstein Publishes the Special Theory of Relativity

Special Theory of Relativity

A lbert Einstein was born in Wurttemberg, Germany on March 14th 1879. He studied Maths and Physics in Germany and then Switzerland. After graduating, Einstein worked in a patent office and it was while working there that he produced his famous equation, the Theory of Relativity. The Theory of Relativity, $E=MC^2$ (E [Energy] is equal to M [Mass] squared by C [The speed of light]), is an equation that proves that mass and energy are different states of the same thing and are interchangeable. The theory shows that neither can be destroyed but under particular circumstances either can be turned into the other.

An example of this can be seen in a star or sun, where the gases are annihilated and turned into light and heat energy. Einstein discovered that all mass in the universe had once been energy given off by the Big Bang.

A new era in physics

Einstein's Theory of Relativity changed the way that scientists considered all matter and also helped them to understand the relationship between time and space. His genius became well-known all around the world and he was invited to work in the USA at Princeton University. He was also given the Nobel Prize for Physics.

Although Einstein was a pacifist, one of the consequences he did not foresee for his Theory of Relativity was the development of nuclear weapons. Nuclear detonation is a method of turning a given mass instantly to heat energy with resulting devastation. In World War Two Einstein believed that the Germans were creating a nuclear weapon and advised the USA to do the same in order to protect themselves. The result was the Manhattan Project, the research programme that ultimately led to the first nuclear attacks on Hiroshima and Nagasaki.

Above: Einstein in 1905 aged 26

Main: Albert Einstein (1879–1955)
German-Swiss-American
mathematician and physicist

1908 Invention of the Model T Ford

Model T Ford

Henry Ford was born into a farming family in Dearborn, near Michigan in June 1863. From childhood he showed an aptitude for mechanics and at the age of 16 set off to work in Detroit as a machinist, servicing and repairing steam engines. He also studied bookkeeping. Whilst in Detroit he married Clara and had a son, Edsel.

In 1891 Ford went to work for the Edison Illuminating Company where his obvious talents earned him rapid promotion. It was here that he first began to put into action his long-held ambition to build a horseless carriage and in 1896 he presented his plans to Thomas Edison himself, who encouraged him to continue. Ford's first car, completed in a tiny workshop in 1896 was called the Ford Quadricycle. It had an ethanol engine and four bicycle wheels.

Designing the first Model T Ford

In the early 20th century, cars were considered a toy for the rich. They were individually made by teams of craftsmen, a method which resulted in vehicles that were 'quirky'. Most cars were not driven by the owner but by a professional chauffeur. Car manufacturers considered that the rich were their only market.

Ford's visionary brilliance, however, led him in a different direction. He aimed to produce a car as cheaply as possible using standard and identical parts for each and every car. In fact, he wanted to produce a car that was cheap enough to be afforded, eventually, by the ordinary person in the street. In 1906 he went to one of his employees, Charles Sorensen, and together they started a process of researching and testing the materials that would eventually be used in their affordable car. They brought in an English metallurgist, J Kent Smith, who showed them vanadium steel, a type of steel that was stronger but easier to work than the steels they had been using.

Above: Driver behind wheel of a 1912 Ford Model T taxi

The assembly line

In October 1908 the first model T was announced. It had two forward gears and a 20 horsepower engine. More importantly it was cheap to build and relatively easy to repair and maintain. Ford's next task was to develop a system of mass production that would reduce the labour costs incumbent on each vehicle to a minimum.

Between 1908 and 1913 he experimented with different production methods, eventually discovering that an assembly line, where the frame of the car was pulled along a different track to different workstations and specialist workers, was the most efficient method of production. This method minimized and organized the movement of people and materials through the plant, and so enabled cars to be constructed more quickly. Soon the production time was halved from twelve hours per car to just six.

Mass production and ownership

In order to fully realize his goal of mass production, Ford moved his company to a new plant at Highland Park which was purpose built to accommodate his assembly line. Engines were constructed on the fourth floor and then along with other parts of the car passed down through the building to the ground floor where they were attached to the chassis. By 1926 fifteen million of the cars had been built and car ownership was no longer the preserve of the very rich.

Henry Ford left two great legacies to the world. He changed the way that car ownership was thought of so that cars could become an everyday item accessible to everyone. Through his pioneering work with assembly line production, he also ushered in an era of more affordable goods of every kind and opened the eyes of the world to the possibilities of large scale industrial manufacturing.

Above: Advertisement for Model T Automobile, circa 1909

1909 Louis Bleriot Flies Across the Channel

The First Aeronautics

Flight has been one of mankind's greatest dreams throughout history with inventors such as Leonardo Da Vinci designing theoretical machines to carry people through the air. In 1903 Orville and Wilbur Wright were the first people to finally achieve this dream with the Wright Flyer, a 12.5 horsepower biplane which was started along a monorail track to build up sufficient speed. The Wright brothers' model required the pilot to lie on the lower wing of the biplane and control the direction using his hips in the same way as a cyclist.

From this limited starting point the race was on for would-be aviators to fly further and higher. Most early plane designs were based on that of the Wright brothers' first successful flyer with an elevator on the nose and propellers to push the plane forwards.

Bleriot's early attempts

Louis Bleriot, born in 1872 near Cambrai, France, started a business making headlamps and other automobile accessories. He used the money he made to research aeronautics and quickly started experimenting with designs for his own plane.

For Bleriot's first attempts at flight he used gliders which were towed along the Seine. He then began to experiment with powered aircraft, first using box-kite biplanes and then tail-first monoplanes similar to those used by the Wright brothers. In 1903 he joined together with fellow inventor Gabriel Voisin and together they worked on designs for a monoplane with a cockpit. Unfortunately they were unsuccessful and parted company when the business began to fail. Inventing solo again, Bleriot created the Bleriot V, the world's first successful monoplane. This model was, however, prone to crashes. In 1909 Bleriot corrected some of the problems of the Bleriot V and completed the Bleriot XI.

Main: Louis Bleriot (1872–1936),
French airman who made the first flight
across the English Channel in 1909

*Right: Bleriot starting the
motor of his monoplane
Bleriot XI 25th July, 1909*

Main: Bleriot after having flown across the Channel

Crossing the channel

The Bleriot XI was a monoplane with a 25 horsepower Anzani engine which used wing warping for stability and forward facing propellers to pull the plane through the air. Bleriot had tested it throughout the summer of 1909 over increasingly long distances.

On July 25th 1909 a race took place to cross the English Channel, a distance of some 23.5 miles. The three aviators taking part were Bleriot, Hubert Latham and Count de Lambert. Neither of the other two could take off due to poor weather conditions. Bleriot had no compass on the Bleriot XI and encountered bad weather conditions and fog as he crossed the channel making it difficult to find the landing site. On the other side, however, he saw a French news reporter waving a French flag and this guided him to the correct place. He landed the plane on target breaking his landing gear in the process, but claiming the £1000 reward from the Daily Mail.

Bleriot's legacy

The ability to fly across a substantial body of water led to a change in thinking about travel and the relative distance between countries. It made trade and travel seem easier, but also made countries feel more vulnerable to attack from the air.

Between 1909 and 1914, in spite of a number of errors which were investigated and corrected by Bleriot himself, 800 planes were made and Bleriot's design was used for the simple fighter planes that were used by Britain, Italy, France, Austria and Russia in World War One. Designs were also built under license by other plane manufacturers in Europe and the USA. Bleriot became one of the leading early pioneers in the mass manufacture of aircraft and continued to manufacture planes in the post war years.

Above: Crowds cheer French aviation pioneer Louis Bleriot (left, waving) at Victoria station, London, after his historic Channel flight

1912 The Sinking of Titanic

Titanic

Making Titanic

In 1912, RMS Titanic was the largest ship in the World and her maiden voyage was a prestigious affair. Constructed at the Harland and Wolff shipyard in Belfast and owned by the White Star line she was built to compete with two Cunard liners, Lusitania and Mauretania, both of which held the Blue Riband for the fastest Atlantic crossing. Titanic and her sister ship Olympic, however, were not built for speed but to carry as many people as possible. In this way they posed a huge commercial threat to the Cunard liners.

Her design was an enlarged version of other, older vessels and some considered that the up-scaled size of Titanic was not quite matched by increased manoeuvrability. In spite of the owner's claims that it was 'practically unsinkable', Titanic had a limited capacity to turn quickly or avoid unexpected objects.

The Maiden Voyage

Titanic left Southampton on April 10th 1912 to begin its five-day crossing to New York. It was carrying more than 2,200 passengers and crew. Captain Edward J Smith was in charge and the Chairman of White Star Line, Bruce Ismay, was also on board as a passenger. The ship took a course across the South Atlantic, a longer crossing than that used by some of her rival cruisers but nevertheless a route that was considered safer and more free of icebergs.

Movies have given us some insight into the way the Titanic looked inside with large, luxurious public dining rooms and first class suites upholstered in fine fabrics with glimmering chandeliers. The second and third class accommodation was more crowded and prosaic and passengers of these classes had their own, more spartan dining rooms and public areas.

Above: Titanic, White Star, Liner on the stocks in Harland & Wolff's shipyard, Belfast, Northern Ireland

Main: The Titanic is being manoeuvred away from Berth 44 in Belfast wharf to begin her maiden voyage, 10th April 1912.

*Above: US Senate inquiry into
the RMS Titanic sinking, 1912*

Catastrophe strikes

There are many myths surrounding the sinking of Titanic,
including one that Ismay encouraged Smith to attempt a
record-breaking crossing on the ship's maiden voyage,
though this has since been debunked.

In fact the blame seems to lie with Captain Smith who failed to
slow the ship in time to avoid an iceberg. On April 15th as Titanic
was nearing the end of her voyage, she struck the iceberg at
around 21 knots and the front six compartments of the ship
filled immediately with icy water. Evacuation procedures
were chaotic with many lifeboats leaving the ship half empty.
In any case the ship was only carrying lifeboats for around
1,200 people owing to a failure by the British Board of Trade.
The only ship to come to Titanic's help was RMS Carphathia
who travelled 93 km off her course to rescue approximately
700 cold, shocked survivors from the scene of the wreck.

The aftermath

The sinking of Titanic was followed by accusations and
investigations. William Randolph Hearst, a powerful newspaper
owner, falsely blamed Bruce Ismay whilst exonerating Captain
Smith. Further accusations were made over White Star Line's
supposed claims that the vessel was 'unsinkable'. Many
surviving crew were interviewed by investigators in an effort
to avoid repeating such a vast loss of life and as a result of
the tragedy evacuation and safety procedures were tightened.

Titanic still lies at the bottom of the Atlantic and divers have
recently discovered fascinating artefacts among the wreck that
tell us about the lives of those who made that fatal voyage.
Today it stands as a memorial to those whose hopes of a new
life in a new country ended before they had even begun. It is
a resting place for those whose stories were cut short by an
unprecedented tragedy.

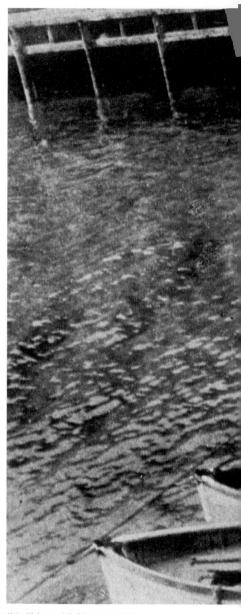

*Main: All that was left of the greatest ship in
the world – the lifeboats that carried most of
the 705 survivors*

Per tutti gli articoli e illustrazioni è riservata la proprietà letteraria e artistica, secondo le leggi e i trattati internazionali.

Anno XVI. — Num. 27.   5 - 12 Luglio 1914.   Centesimi 10 il numero.

L'assassinio a Serajevo dell'arciduca Francesco Ferdinando erede del trono d'Austria, e di sua moglie.

Main: Achille Beltrame's illustration of assassination of Archduke
Franz Ferdinand, heir to the Austrian throne, and his wife

1914 The Assassination of Archduke Franz Ferdinand

Franz Ferdinand Assassination

Europe and the Balkans

As the 20th Century entered its second decade trouble was brewing in the Balkans. Previously governed by the Ottoman Empire, the southern Slavic region of Bosnia-Herzegovina had wanted to unite with ambitious and nationalistic Serbia, but instead was annexed in 1908 by the large and powerful Austro-Hungarian Empire. The annexation was unpopular in Serbia and Bosnia and nationalist groups sprang up. One such nationalist group was the Black Hand.

In 1914 there was a tentative peace in Europe but international relations were dominated by a system of alliances. The Austro-Hungarian Empire was closely allied to Germany, whilst Russia, a supporter of Serbia, was allied to France and Britain. The German Kaiser, Wilhelm II, had created enmity amongst the British and French with his aggressive expansionist policies.

Archduke Franz Ferdinand visits Sarajevo

On 28th June 1914 Archduke Franz Ferdinand, the heir to the Austrian throne, had scheduled a visit to Sarajevo in order to inspect imperial troops. The date itself was sensitive being the anniversary of Serbia's defeat by the Ottomans so a visit by the representative of a new occupying power on the same date could have been considered ill-advised. The Archduke was in any case unpopular in Bosnia as he had promised 'changes' when he acceded the throne.

The Archduke was accompanied by his pregnant wife Sophie, and the date also coincided with their wedding anniversary. As the daughter of a poor Czech aristocrat Sophie was not allowed to appear in public with her husband at home in Austria, but in Sarajevo, an annexed territory, protocol allowed her to sit alongside him.

*Above: The arrest of Gavrilo Princip
(1895–1918), the assassin, at the scene*

Above: Danilo Ilitch, the Balkan anarchist who was tried for organizing the Sarajevo assassination of Franz Ferdinand

The assassination

When the Archduke and his wife arrived they toured Sarajevo in an open car with little security. Three terrorists from the Black Hand Serbian nationalist group were waiting in the crowd with grenades. Two of the grenades could not be used as the crowd was too dense but the leader of the terrorists, Nedjelko Cabrinovic, released a grenade which landed on the back of the car but then rolled off, injuring a security officer and some bystanders. The car continued on its way with the royal couple unhurt.

Later on, the Archduke and his wife set off to visit their injured security man. The car took a wrong turn by Appel Quay, by chance passing another Black Hand member, Gavrilo Princip. The 19 year old Serbian terrorist fired a pistol twice, first hitting Sophie in the stomach, and then the Archduke himself in the neck. Both victims died within an hour and Princip was arrested and later imprisoned.

The war begins

Catastrophically, the assassination of the Archduke was the small spark that set alight the dry tinderbox of Europe's troubled relations. Austria-Hungary blamed Serbia for the assassination, but also saw it as an opportunity to subdue Serbian nationalism once and for all by means of defeat. On July 28th Austria declared war on Serbia. Serbia, however, was supported by the Russians who in turn declared war on Austria-Hungary. Germany sprang to defend and support Austria-Hungary as its closest ally and almost immediately after that France and Britain lined up with the Russians.

So the diplomatic battle lines were drawn and real battle was soon to follow. Even in the turbulent waters of the Balkans in 1914 no one could have predicted the scale of war that would follow as a result of the actions of one nineteen-year-old boy.

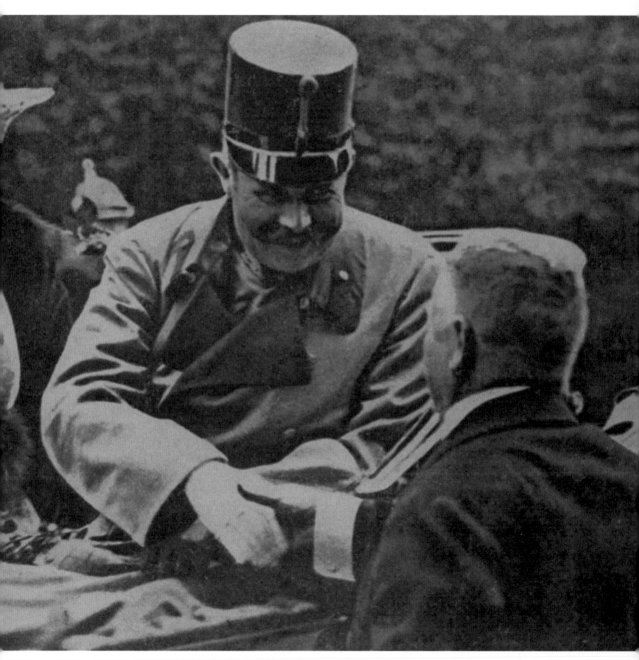

Main: Franz Ferdinand and his wife Sophie in Sarajevo moments before their assassination

1915 The Sinking of Lusitania

Lusitania

The war at sea

By 1915 most of Europe was embroiled in what would become known as World War One, although the Americans remained neutral. While the battle over land raged in Belgium and France the war at sea had a different character. The British Navy maintained an increasingly tight blockade to prevent essential supplies from reaching Germany in an attempt to bring the German command to its knees. As the blockade started to bite, the Germans retaliated by sending their U-boats to sink British merchant and even civilian vessels.

Submarines, or U-boats as the Germans called them, had been built by the British and the Germans before the start of

the war. Britain had greater naval strength and numbers than the Germans but the Germans learned to deploy their U-boats with increasing menace which made those travelling to and from Britain by sea feel threatened.

Submarines, or U-boats as the Germans called them, had been built by the British and the Germans before the start of the war. Britain had greater naval strength and numbers than the Germans but the Germans learned to deploy their U-boats with increasing menace which made those travelling to and from Britain by sea feel threatened.

Above: Sinking of the American liner Lusitania after being struck by a torpedo from a German submarine

Lusitania

Before the war began, RMS Lusitania was one of the fastest cruising ships in the world travelling at an average 25 knots. A beautiful and refined vessel with elegant public areas and luxurious suites, she held the Blue Riband for the fastest Atlantic crossing. In 1913 she had been secretly fitted with ammunition magazines and gun mounts in anticipation of the need to use her as a fighting ship at the outbreak of war. In 1915 she was still, however, operating her usual passenger route from British ports to New York although passenger numbers were well down.

Unknown to her passengers she was also being used to transport small arms and ammunition to be used for trench warfare currently raging around Europe. To the German U-boats this secondary use made her fair game for an attack.

Above: Illustration of the sinking of the Lusitania by a German submarine showing crew and passengers struggling to get into lifeboats

Above: World War One, Irish propaganda poster showing the Lusitania in flames
and sinking, with people in the water and lifeboats in the foreground

Lusitania is Torpedoed

Lusitania set out from New York on 1st May 1915 carrying almost 2,000 passengers and crew. Under the control of Captain Turner, she was twelve miles off the southern coast of Ireland on May 7th when a German U-boat, U-20, commanded by Captain Schweiger, sent a torpedo ripping into her side. The initial strike was followed moments later by a second explosion which tore the ship apart. Unlike the sinking of Titanic which took three hours, Lusitania went down in a matter of minutes and eyewitnesses reported scenes of chaos with lifeboats falling into the sea nose first or crashing onto the deck because of the angle of the ship.

The cause of the second explosion has long been debated. It may have been the result of the torpedo rupturing a fuel tank but some believe it could have come from explosives that were being carried secretly in the ship's hold, bound for the British troops.

USA joins the war

Almost 1,200 people were killed on Lusitania of whom 128 were American. This loss of life had a huge impact on the Americans who considered it an injustice that their people should suffer when they were not at war. President Wilson complained to the Germans who accepted responsibility and said that they would only attack passenger ships in future with prior warning. A storm of outrage, however, swept the USA and the rest of the world and relations between the USA and Germany soured. In 1917 America declared war on Germany bringing a level of military might and manpower which the German army could not resist.

The intervention of the USA in World War One eventually brought the war to its conclusion in the Allies' favour. Had Lusitania not been torpedoed on May 7th 1915 the outcome of the war could have been very different.

Above: Front page of the New York Herald newspaper

1916 The First Day of the Battle of the Somme

Somme

Trench warfare

World War One was characterized by the difficulty and high human cost which accompanied almost all advances. In each of the major battles, both sides dug and occupied trenches which faced each other across no-man's land, and were large enough to conceal soldiers from sniper fire and shelling until the inevitable orders came to go over the top and advance on the enemy. Trench conditions were riddled with the smell of death and the volunteer soldiers who sat in them waiting for orders to advance could never have anticipated the squalid conditions in which they would fight.

As 1916 dawned, allied troops were locked in a stalemate with their German counterparts with each side making only tiny advances against the enemy. Even such small victories either side achieved were very quickly lost or reversed. The British Commander in Chief, Douglas Haig, wanted a significant breakthrough.

Above: Battle of the Somme, France, 1916, A German soldier wearing a gas mask about to hurl a hand-grenade from a trench

Main: Roll call of the 1st Battalion, Lancashire Fusiliers on the afternoon of 1st July 1916

A major offensive

Haig and his French counterpart Joffre had been planning a major joint offensive since late 1915. The area decided upon was an area stretching around 30 km to the north and south of the Somme. The intention was to break through enemy lines and advance through the French countryside. The purpose and timing of the battle plan began to change, however, owing to events at Verdun.

In early 1916 the German Army Chief of Staff, von Falkenhayn, attacked the town of Verdun, an ancient fortified town important to the French. He knew that the French would fight hard to defend it and so focused all his efforts on his defeat, aiming to 'bleed the French white'. He had almost succeeded in breaching the final fortress in June 1916 when Commander Joffre persuaded Haig to bring the battle of the Somme a month earlier than planned. The battle of the Somme began on 1st July, forcing German troops away from Verdun and relieving the French.

The bloodiest day

On 24th of June, Haig instructed heavy artillery bombardment of the German lines. This was intended to clear the way for an easy advance. The bombardment was followed by a creeping barrage that would precede the infantry advance to the front line. Haig did not conceal preparations for the advance and the bombardment itself was something of a giveaway. The German troops knew well what was coming and stayed in their well constructed concrete bunkers where they were relatively unaffected by the bombardment.

On July 1st the whistle was blown for the infantry advance to begin. Eleven British divisions north of the Somme and five French divisions south of the Somme were ordered to walk slowly across no-man's land. The Germans, however, were ready with machine guns and the slaughter began at once. There were 60,000 British casualties on the first day of the battle, of which around 20,000 were deaths. It remains the highest loss of life in a single day of battle.

A futile battle

For weeks after the first day of the Somme, British newspapers were filled with the names of those dead, lost and injured. It quickly became apparent that the intended big breakthrough was in fact a failure. The only area where advances could be made was in the area south of the Somme where the French had been stationed, but even here any advances could not be consolidated. In November, following heavy downpours, the battle was called off with a total Allied advance of just eight kilometres.

The Battle of the Somme became synonymous with futile loss of life. It has also come to symbolize the vast difference in perspective between the war generals who give orders far from the field of battle, and the ordinary soldiers who carry out their orders and pay the ultimate price.

Above: A heavy shell exploding during the Battle of the Somme

Main: Soldiers moving forward through wire at the start of the Battle of the Somme, 1st July 1916

Main: British troops
go over the top of the
trenches during the Battle
of the Somme, 1916

1917 The First Tank Battle

Tank Battles

The need for a breakthrough

As World War One ground on with little progress on either side, commanders realized that they would have to be more creative if they wanted to make any kind of major breakthrough on land. Cavalry was useless on the quagmires that each battlefield had now become, and the relentless attrition of trench warfare could not continue indefinitely. Commanders and politicians began to consider more seriously how armoured vehicles could be used to help the war effort.

The biggest supporters of the introduction of armoured vehicles were Lieutenant-Colonel Ernest Swinton and Maurice Hankey, secretary of the Committee for Imperial Defence. They saw that a vehicle was needed that could move on any terrain, however muddy and uneven. Such vehicles had been in use by Britain and Germany before the outbreak of World War One but they were only designed to work on flat terrain. The new design would need to be more innovative.

Above: An American soldier walks ahead of an MKIV British-made tank

Designing the tanks

In 1915, a year after the war had started, Swinton organized a demonstration of the Killen-Strait tractor, an engine on caterpillar tracks, which successfully demonstrated its ability to cut through barbed wire defences. Those present at the demonstration, including future Prime Ministers Lloyd George and Winston Churchill, were impressed with its potential. A committee was established to design and build the new weapons.

The specifications were:

- A top speed of 4 mph
- Ability to turn quickly at top speed
- Ability to climb a 5-foot parapet
- Ability to cross an eight-foot gap
- A 20 mile operating radius.

William Foster and Walter Tritton were commissioned to produce the first 'landship' (as it was then known), in secrecy. The machine they built was nicknamed 'Big Willie'. It had a Daimler engine, weighed fourteen tons and had twelve foot long track frames. It could hold three men in cramped conditions and travelled at 2mph in battlefield conditions.

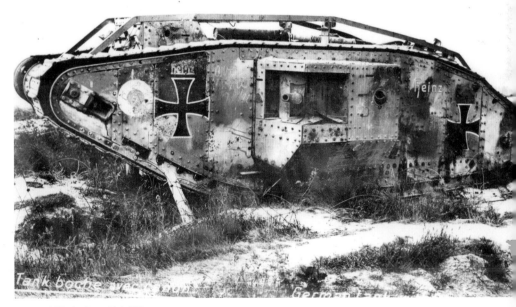

Above: World War One German Tank, 1917

Above: An early American Army tank

The first major tank battle

The 'landship' eventually came to be known informally as the 'tank' owing to its similarity in shape to a water tank, but the name stuck. The new design tank was deployed initially in September 1916, and later at Flers near the Somme. These earliest outings were not entirely successful as the tanks were unreliable, some breaking down and others becoming stuck in muddy ditches.

The first major, successful use of the tank was at the Battle of Cambrai on November 20th 1917, when the entire British Tank Corps, some 474 tanks, swept the Germans aside capturing 10,000 men and many weapons although there was insufficient infantry available to consolidate this advantage. The Battle of Cambrai established the tank's usefulness in battle and the Germans and Americans quickly began work on their own designs.

Above: Battle between Allied and German tanks in May 1918

Tanks fighting tanks

By April 1918 the Germans had their own version of the tank and at Villers Bretonneux 13 of these engaged in battle with British and Australian infantry. This became famous as the first battle between tanks, although three British Mark IVs eventually drove off the German A7Vs.

Throughout 1918 tanks came to be used increasingly ahead of infantry to ensure a swift and safe advance for men on foot and avoiding pointless waste of life. General Monash, head of the Australian corps, perfected this art when he took victory at La Hamel in just 93 minutes. By the end of the war the British had made over 2,500 tanks and the French almost 4,000. In spite of their reputation for engineering the Germans made just 20. The increased mobility, safety for troops and sheer brute force that the tanks provided was a decisive factor in the Allied victory of World War One.

Right: Charles Augustus Lindbergh (1902–1974), and the 'Spirit of St Louis', the plane he flew for the first non-stop solo flight across the Atlantic

1921–1940

1927 Charles Lindbergh Flies the Atlantic Solo

Flying the Atlantic

Aviator Charles Lindbergh

Charles Lindbergh was born in Detroit on 4th February 1902. He grew up in Little Falls, Minnesota, and showed exceptional mechanical ability from an early age. At the age of eighteen he went to the University of Wisconsin to study engineering. After two years, however, he left to become a barnstormer or stunt pilot. He was fascinated by the new technology of aviation and wanted to be at the cutting edge of new developments.

In 1924 he signed up to be an Army Air Reserve Pilot for the United States Army. When he graduated in 1925 he was considered the best pilot in class. He was quickly hired by the Robertson Aircraft Corporation to fly the mail from Chicago to St Louis.

Above: Lindbergh's departure for Paris

The spirit of St Louis

In 1919 a New York hotel owner called Raymond Orteig offered a reward of $25,000 for the first pilot who could make a solo crossing of the Atlantic. Several pilots had tried and failed and some had even given their lives but in 1927 the reward had still not been claimed. Lindbergh believed that he could win the reward provided he had the right plane. Securing financial support from nine St Louis businessmen, Lindbergh asked the Ryan Aeronautical Company to build him a special plane which he helped to design himself.

The name of the plane which in time became a global phenomenon was The Spirit of St Louis. Lindbergh tested it by flying from San Diego to New York City in just twenty hours and twenty-one minutes, a trans-continental record.

New York to Paris

On 20th May, 1927 at 7.52am, The Spirit of St Louis took off from Roosevelt Field, Long Island, New York. A heavy plane loaded with 450 gallons of fuel, the plane only just cleared the telephone wires at the end of the runway. The route would take Lindbergh north towards Nova Scotia and then across the Atlantic, eventually landing in Paris.

Lindbergh felt tired after only four hours in the plane and found himself falling asleep with his eyes open for a couple of minutes at a time. Equipped with only a magnetic compass and his flight charts, Lindbergh's navigation proved surprisingly accurate and twenty-seven hours into his flight, when he sighted the Irish coast, he was just three miles off course. The thought of landing in Paris seems to have kept Lindbergh going for the last exhausting hours of his flight. When he landed at Le Bourget aerodrome, Paris, at 10.22pm he had been flying for thirty-three and a half hours.

A new aviation era

Charles Lindbergh's epic solo flight caught the imagination of the entire world. People waited by their radios in Europe and the USA to hear whether Lindbergh would succeed and when he landed in Paris he was greeted as a hero. The psychological impact of the crossing was to make the World seem a smaller and more accessible place, a process which has continued ever since. Lindbergh's Atlantic crossing was also an enormous global media event in which he was catapulted to immediate celebrity status.

Lindbergh's impact on aeronautics did not end there. After the Atlantic crossing he flew widely across the USA supporting the Guggenheim fund which was dedicated to aeronautic research. He persuaded the Guggenheim family to support Professor Robert Goddard, a scientist whose work was instrumental in the development of satellites, missiles and space travel.

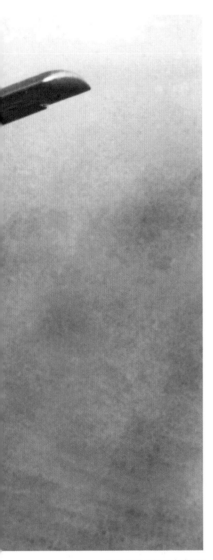

Above: Lindbergh was the first to cross the Atlantic from West to East in 33 hours and 30 minutes

Above: Colonel Lindbergh was welcomed as a hero in New York at the beginning of June 1927

Main: Al Jolson in The Jazz Singer

1927 The First Talking Picture

Talking Pictures

Above: The cast on set during the filming of The Jazz Singer

Silent movies

Even before the 20th century had begun, Thomas Edison had started to experiment with adding sound to film. He found the process of synchronizing the speech and the picture, however, too difficult and so the 'silent movie' was born. Silent movies, where actors told stories with exaggerated movements and facial expressions, were accompanied by subtitles to tell the story and backing music to convey the atmosphere of each scene.

Silent movies were popular in the early 20th century and through the First World War and some of the actors are still well known to this day. Two of the greatest silent actors were Charlie Chaplin and Buster Keaton. Charlie Chaplin's ability to make comedy from movement and expression is still considered by many to be the most highly accomplished comedy acting, whilst Buster Keaton's film The General is a masterpiece of comedy and suspense.

The first 'talkie'

In the 1920s filmmakers began once again to consider how sound and pictures could be recorded together and broadcast simultaneously. In 1925 Western Electric and Warner Brothers agreed to produce a system for making movies with sound. The system, called Vitaphone and invented by Bell Laboratories, was a way of recording sound onto the filmstrip itself. The first movie to make use of their system was Don Juan in 1926. In Don Juan the story was told in the usual way with gestures and subtitles but singing and music were recorded as part of the film.

The breakthrough with speech came one year later on 6th October 1927 when Warner Brothers released the first film to include synchronized speech. The film was called The Jazz Singer.

AL JOLSON in "THE JAZZ SINGER" with May McAvoy   A WARNER BROS. PRODUCTION   MADE IN U.S.A.

Above: Al Jolson in a scene from The Jazz Singer

The Jazz Singer

The Jazz Singer is a film about Jakie, the son of a Jewish cantor. Jakie, played by 1920s superstar Al Jolson, wants to leave home to become a jazz musician but to do so he must go against his father's wishes. After years of playing jazz in clubs and bars he meets a famous performer, Mary Dale, who helps him and soon he is offered a show on Broadway. At the climax of the film he must make a choice whether to continue with the show or visit his dying father.

Sam Warner was intending to record The Jazz Singer in the same way as Don Juan but Jolson ad-libbed a few lines of speech just before one of his songs. The producers liked the ad-lib and kept it in the final film. The first spoken words on film were, 'Wait a minute! Wait a minute! You ain't heard nothin' yet.'

Talkies take over

Jolson's first broadcast words proved strangely prophetic. The public hadn't heard anything yet but soon they would hear more. By 1930 almost all films were talkies and some films such as All Quiet on the Western Front were produced with a silent and a talkie version so that cinemas with no sound facilities and cinemas in non-English speaking countries could show them. A new line-up of big stars appeared such as Greta Garbo and Douglas Fairbanks Jr. Jolson himself went on to become a legend of American cinema.

The development of sound in film ushered in a new and exciting era of movie making which has entertained and educated audiences around the globe for most of the last century. Films and film stars are part of our lives and film makers are still looking for the next Big Thing in technology to entice their global audience.

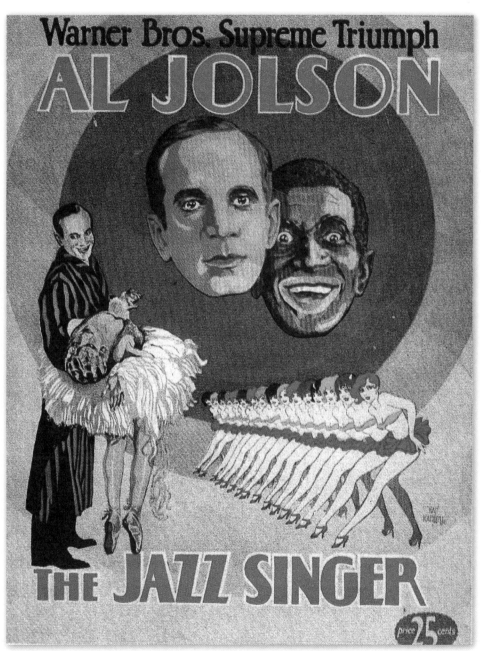

Above: Film poster for The Jazz Singer

1928 Alexander Fleming Discovers Penicillin

Penicillin Discovery

Before antibiotics

In the early 20th century scientists knew that many diseases and health problems were caused by the spread of bacteria. People could sometimes die as the result of simple injuries from tetanus or gangrene, where bacteria would grow in a wound and spread quickly to the rest of the body. The problem of bacterial infection was never more apparent than in World War One where many soldiers injured on the battlefield were treated in insanitary field hospitals with other sick patients and bacteria could spread back and forth.

One doctor who saw the problems of disease and infection first hand was a doctor Alexander Fleming, a researcher at St Mary's hospital in London.

Alexander Fleming

Alexander Fleming ranks alongside Edward Jenner and Louis Pasteur as one of the great discoverers of medical history. Born into a farming family in Ayrshire in 1881, he moved to London at the age of thirteen and later began to train as a doctor. In 1906 he graduated from medical school with distinction and began work as a researcher at St Mary's hospital Medical School. His mentor there was Sir Almroth Wright, who was a leading pioneer of vaccine therapy.

During World War One Fleming signed up to work on the Western Front as a medic where he was mentioned in dispatches. After the war he returned to work at St Mary's where he continued to be fascinated by bacteria and immunology.

Above: Sir Alexander Fleming (1881–1955) in his laboratory at St Mary's Hospital, Paddington

Main: Fleming shared the 1945 Nobel Prize for Physiology or Medicine with the two chemists who had perfected a method of producing penicillin

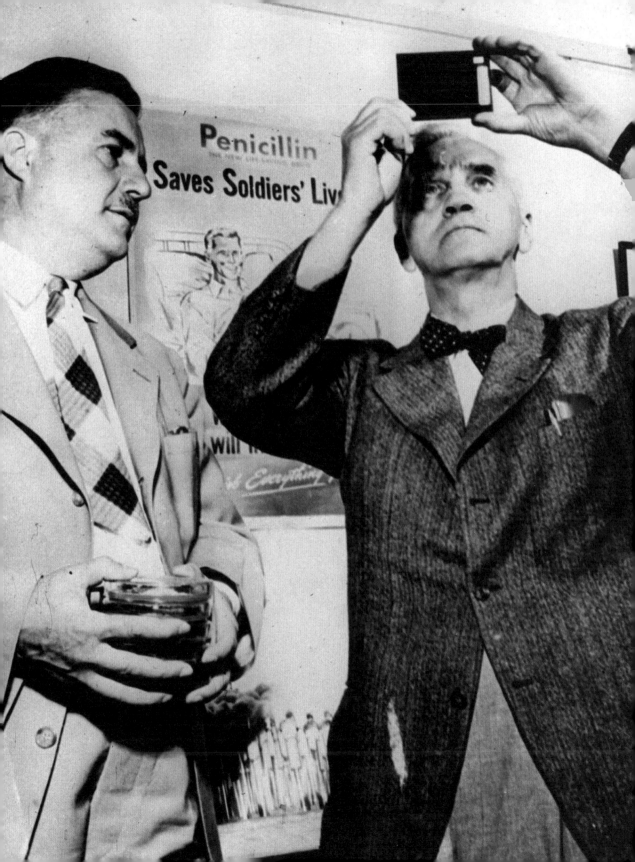

Penicillin is discovered

Fleming's breakthrough in the discovery of penicillin came almost by accident. He had been on holiday and on return had found his laboratory cluttered. Sorting through some glass plates he discovered that some he had been working on, which had been coated with staphylococcus bacteria, had not been cleaned. A circle of mould had started to grow on one of them.

When Fleming looked closely at the plate on his microscope he discovered that the staphylococcus bacteria had disappeared from the area surrounding the mouldy growth. Fleming hypothesized that a substance in the mould had killed the bacteria. Further research on the mold discovered that it could kill off other bacteria and could even be given to small animals without any side effects. The mould was penicillin notatum.

Penicillin is developed as an antibiotic

Fleming moved on to other work without fully realizing the value of what he had discovered but about ten years later two scientists working at Oxford University, Ernst Chain and Edward Florey, picked up where Fleming had left off and isolated the bacteria-killing substance penicillin. Soon after, in 1941, Dr Charles Fletcher heard of their work and wanted to try penicillin on a patient who was close to dying from an infected wound. The patient's wound healed impressively although the patient subsequently died owing to the extent of the infection.

Penicillin had clear potential as a 'wonder drug'. The Second World War was by then in full swing so demand for the drug was high and By D-Day in 1944 enough penicillin had been produced to care for soldiers injured in the fighting. In the post-war era penicillin and other antibiotics have transformed modern healthcare and saved uncountable lives.

Above: Sir Alexander Fleming sits next to a collection of test-tubes and dishes, in his laboratory

Main: Portrait of Professor Alexander Fleming from 1934

1929 The Wall Street Crash

Wall Street Crash

Boom time

After the First World War the USA entered a phase of unprecedented prosperity and consumerism known as the Roaring Twenties. There was an abundance of new technology such as the motor car, the airplane and radios. Jobs were readily available and unemployment was low. A new middle class emerged that could afford domestic luxuries and enjoy entertainments such as jazz music and cinema visits.

New companies sprang up, funding themselves sometimes by floating shares on the stock market. New buildings appeared, such as the Empire State, and cities like New York and Chicago grew rapidly as they became centres for industry and innovation. In 1928 President Hoover declared that the USA was 'nearer to the final triumph over poverty than ever before in the history of any land'. He could not have known how wrong he would turn out to be.

Right: Traders working in Wall Street, in New York, 1929

Above: Crowds massed outside the New York stock exchange during the Wall Street crash

The first signs of trouble

Not everything, however, was quite as good as it seemed. Farmers had got into the habit of producing as much as they could during the World War One, with the result that by the mid-1920s supply outstripped demand and prices fell, as did the price of land. Demand for new consumer goods also fell. This was partly owing to market saturation but also because new export duties imposed by other countries in retaliation to the USA's import tariffs meant that the USA could export fewer goods to the rest of the World.

As goods came to be worth less, so too did the companies that made them. Throughout the 1920s people had started to buy more and more shares creating an overheated market and a bubble in prices. Events came to a head in October 1929 when suddenly the bubble burst.

Main: *Little after the Crash of Wall Street on 24th October, 1929, crowds of speculators and stockholders gathered before the Paris Stock Exchange*

Above: The front page of the Brooklyn Daily Eagle

Above: Messengers from brokerage houses seem unconcerned as they learn about the crash

Black Monday

On 28th October 1929 the US stock market went into free fall as investors tried desperately to sell their shares. The market lost 30% of its value in the following week and banks and wealthy investors such as Rockefeller poured money into the economy in an effort to save it. Millions of savers had their shares wiped out. Businesses and banks went bankrupt and within three years unemployment in the USA rose from 1.5 million to 12.8 million.

Many people lost their homes and lived in Hoovervilles, makeshift villages with houses made of debris, and countless people lived on the verge of starvation in primitive conditions. One family in New York lived in a cave in Central Park, and children were deserted as their parents were either too poor or too sick to care for them. The impact on the stock market was felt around the World.

The long road to recovery

Overall, the market dropped 89% by 1932, by which time one quarter of the population was unemployed. Not only the USA but the World went into a general depression with high unemployment and falling prices. European banks were also pushed to the brink as the USA recalled its loans and the severity of the resulting slump in Germany was a considerable help to the small but ambitious National Socialist party, led by Adolf Hitler.

In the USA, the Wall Street Crash changed forever the way that banks were run. Franklin D Roosevelt brought in new financial legislation to regulate the banks' behaviour and he also introduced a government run social welfare program for the first time in the USA. Possibly the biggest change to come about, however, as a result of the Wall Street Crash was a permanent end to the financial naivety and over-confidence of the Roaring Twenties.

1930 Gandhi Completes the Salt March

Salt March

The Raj

From 1858 until 1947 the British Empire controlled India during a time known as the British Raj. During the Raj, Britain controlled trade between India and itself in a way that was often more beneficial to Britain. For example, cash crops such as cotton and tea were grown in abundance in India to be sold in Britain but as a result India found itself with famine on its hands as insufficient food crops were grown to feed its vast population.

One of the most unjust aspects of trade was the Salt Acts. These made it illegal for Indians to produce or collect salt for themselves and forced them to buy it instead, even though it was a mineral that was readily available on beaches and essential to the Indian diet. The Salt Acts affected the poor more than any other group in society since it forced unnecessary expense on them and as such was considered highly unjust.

Who was Gandhi?

Mohandas Gandhi was born in Kathiawar, India on 2nd October 1869. He studied law in England and then spent two decades in South Africa where he fought discrimination against Indian settlers with his philosophy of Satyagraha, or non-violent protest.

In 1914 he returned to India and joined the Home Rule movement. He became leader of the Indian National Congress where he expressed his aim to alleviate the suffering of poor farm workers and labourers brought about by unjust British taxation. He also had a wider social vision, wishing to bring an end to the caste system, liberate women and establish a simpler and fairer way of life for all Indians. He believed that Satyagraha, the philosophy he pioneered in South Africa, could help to bring this about.

Above: Mohandas Gandhi (4L) walking with followers on the Salt March toward Dandi

Main: Young Gandhi, taken in 1887

Above: Gandhi arrives in Delhi in 1930

The Salt march

In 1930 Gandhi decided that the Salt Acts would be his rallying call for civil disobedience. He wrote to the Viceroy and warned that if the Salt Acts were not revoked, he would begin a 240 mile march to the sea where he and his supporters would illegally collect salt. On March 12th he began the march with 78 fellow Satyagrahis. Gandhi spoke at each village he passed and gathered more supporters on the way.

When they reached the coast 23 days later Gandhi picked up a lump of salt from the beach and in doing so immediately defied the law. His supporters followed suit. Arrests immediately followed, including the arrest of Gandhi himself a month later but the seed of civil disobedience was sown and more salt marches followed around the country.

Independence

On 21st May 1930, 2,500 people marched on the Dharasana Salt Works North of Mumbai (Bombay). The protest was peaceful but was met with violent opposition from the police and many protesters were killed on the spot although they offered no physical resistance. The incident caused an outcry around the world. On his release from prison in 1931 Gandhi called off the Satyagraha but was granted a place at the negotiating table in London to discuss India's future. Nothing was immediately resolved but Gandhi's power to change world opinion had been acknowledged.

Home Rule for India did not follow until 1947 but Gandhi's lofty minded ideal of peaceful protest, of not sinking to the level of your oppressor, has become one of the guiding principles of those seeking to overturn injustice.

Above: A Statue Of Gandhi In Tavistock Square, London

1936 Jesse Owens, Olympic Champion

Jesse Owens

A divided society

In the early half of the twentieth century black people in Europe and the USA were treated as second-class citizens or worse. In the American Deep South where Jesse Owens was born, African Americans were segregated by law so that they could not attend the same schools, shops or even cinemas as white people. Many black people worked as tenant farmers constantly working to pay rent to white owners. In Alabama, black men suspected of crimes were lynched before they could be legally tried for a crime, but even if brought to trial they were unlikely to be treated unfairly.

Opportunities for black people were more limited than for their white counterparts and the odds were stacked against black children who showed extraordinary talent.

Jesse Owens

Born on September 12th 1913 to a tenant farmer in Alabama, James Cleveland Owens began helping to pick cotton at the age of seven. Soon after, he moved with his family to Cleveland, Ohio where he received a better education than in Alabama. He showed early promise as an athlete at East Technical High School where he made a name for himself as a sprinter, setting records in the 100 and 200-yard dash as well as the long jump.

He went on to study at Ohio State University where in the 1935 Big Ten championships he equalled the record for the 100-yard dash and set a record in the long jump that was to last for 25 years. In 1935 he entered 42 events and won them all including three at the Olympic trials. The stage was set for the most important contest of all.

Above: Owens won 4 gold medals: 100 m, 200 m, 4x100 m and long jump

Above: Jesse Owens (1913 –1980) at the 1936 Berlin Olympics

*Above: Owens crosses the finish
line first in the 200 m final*

The 1936 Berlin Olympics

Adolf Hitler had intended that the 1936 Olympic Games
in Berlin would showcase German and Aryan (white,
fair-haired) supremacy. He was critical of the Americans
for including black athletes in their team. The games,
however, did not turn out at all as Hitler had planned.
In all, the USA gained eleven gold medals, six of them
going to black athletes. Of these, Jesse Owens was by far
the most successful, gaining four gold medals in the 100
metres, 200 metres, 400 metre relay and the long jump.

A furious Hitler is said to have stormed out of the stadium
although Owens, a mild-mannered and generous man,
has said that Hitler later congratulated him. His own
president Franklin D Roosevelt, however, never invited
Owens to the White House or publicly congratulated
him as would have been considered usual for such a
significant champion.

Slow change

Sadly Owens' success at the World's most prestigious
sporting event did little to change things back home or
in Germany. When he went home to Ohio he still had to
use back doors, sit at the back of the bus and live in the
areas of town reserved for black people. His achievement
was not officially recognized by the USA until 1976 when
Gerald Ford awarded him the Presidential Medal
of Freedom.

Owens and the other black athletes did, however,
challenge the prevailing attitude to black people. They
made Hitler look like a fool for believing his 'Master Race'
was physically superior and they made a mockery of racial
segregation laws in their own country. They were cheered
as Americans by the rest of the World and it would
become increasingly difficult to ignore and marginalize
black Americans as a result of their success.

*Right: Owens salutes the American flag
during his gold medal ceremony*

1940 Nazi Blitzkrieg on the Western Front

The Nazis

The Nazis prepare for war

Since 1933 when the Nazi party under Adolf Hitler was elected to rule in Germany they had been governed by defining principles of aggressive nationalism. They made no secret of their desire to reclaim lands taken from them under the Treaty of Versailles at the close of World War One, but their plans for expansion did not end there. They considered the other countries of Europe fair game for occupation as well in order that the dream of establishing a 'Master Race' could succeed.

Hitler had been preparing hard for the outbreak of World War Two. He had begun compulsory conscription in 1936 and with his four-year plans had vastly increased the country's supply of raw materials and its ability to remain self-sufficient. He had also been stockpiling weapons so that they could be deployed swiftly and with devastating impact.

The tactic of Blitzkrieg

Before the outbreak of World War Two, an army officer called Hans Guderian wrote a pamphlet on battle strategy called 'Achtung Panzer'. In it he outlined a tactic which he called 'Blitzkrieg' or 'lightning war'. In his pamphlet he claimed it would be possible to attack a target such as France and reach the coast within a matter of weeks. The Blitzkrieg method was to move swiftly using light armoured tanks, supported by infantry and aircraft. First of all planes would carry out strategic bombing to destroy communication points and railways, and before those under attack had found time to organize themselves, tanks would roll in to take over one town at a time.

To be successful, Blitzkrieg needed to be highly organized and coordinated. Hitler saw Guderian's pamphlet and wanted to put it into action although some of his generals were sceptical.

Above: Officers of the German High Command including Luftwaffe chief Hermann Goering, 2nd right studying maps on the western front

Left: German Fuhrer Adolf Hitler takes the salute at the Berlin Olympic Games in 1936

Main: German soldiers prepare to support a river crossing
with light machine gun fire on the western

Blitzkrieg in action

Poland was to be the first country to feel the full force of Blitzkrieg. On 1st September 1939 two German armies attacked Poland, one in the north and one in the south. It took just five days to destroy the Polish air force and by the end of September Poland had surrendered.

The attack on the Netherlands, Belgium, Luxembourg and France began on May 10th 1940 and within six weeks all four countries had been defeated, with British and French troops evacuated at Dunkirk. The Allied troops were superior in number to the Germans, but the German preparation for Blitzkrieg meant that the German Luftwaffe were greater in number and more effective than those of their allied counterparts. They also made better use of their tank divisions which surged ahead of the German infantry forcing the speed of the advance and leaving the allies with no chance to organise a response.

Above: A German armoured observation car and its crew on the western front

Dunkirk

Over 330,000 British and French troops were eventually trapped on the beaches at Dunkirk, having been driven back by the Germans. They were surrounded by the German army who waited for the order to begin an all-out attack. The order to begin an attack never came but the beach was bombed by the Luftwaffe and many soldiers died as they waited for transport. A rescue party of 800 little ships was sent to carry the soldiers from the beach to larger ships that were anchored further out to sea.

As the humiliated British troops fled the beaches of Dunkirk and France surrendered to Germany it seemed as though defeat for the Allies and the other countries of Europe could be the only outcome. New ways of fighting would need to be found in the air and on land if the Allies were to have a hope of defeating Hitler.

1941–1960

1941 Operation Barbarossa

Barbarossa

A false promise

In 1939 Hitler and Stalin signed a pact of non-aggression, agreeing that neither side would attack the other for ten years. The agreement was false on both sides. Hitler wanted to consolidate his attack on the Western Front before embarking on a Soviet invasion and Stalin needed time to revitalize his forces and train new and loyal Red Army commanders following the purges of the 1930s. Stalin, a paranoid leader who constantly feared threats to his position, had damaged his own army by imprisoning or executing many of his most experienced generals.

Hitler hated the USSR. He considered all Eastern Europeans as 'untermenschen' or 'sub-human' and he believed they had no right to occupy the lands that they did. To make matters worse, the USSR was communist and Hitler hated communism, so the USSR was a primary target.

Planning Barbarossa

Barbarossa, the plan made by Hitler to invade The Soviet Union, was planned through the closing months of 1940 and several versions were drawn up. The final version which Hitler approved focused on three main targets which were Leningrad in the North, Moscow in the centre and Kiev to the South. Moscow and Leningrad were considered the biggest targets. The German attack force comprised three million soldiers, 3580 tanks and 1830 planes and was the largest army ever assembled to fight against the largest country in the World.

Having seen Blitzkrieg work so well on the Western Front and knowing that the Russian, or Red Army was in poor shape, Hitler was convinced that victory would come easily. He believed he would only have to 'kick in the front door and the whole rotten Soviet edifice will come tumbling down'.

Above: Operation Barbarossa, German soldiers in armoured vehicle of the Wehrmacht are approaching a burning Russian truck

Main: Two soldiers with a light 5 cm mortar

Above: Wehrmacht troops are moving deeper into
Russia in 1942; they were part of over 4.5 million troops
of the Axis powers during the invasion of the USSR

Above: A Wehrmacht soldier is guarding a village under the snow

Massive force

Using Blitzkrieg and a massive attack force, Hitler was very nearly proved right. The attack started at 3am on 22nd June 1941. By day 17 of the attack, 300,000 Soviets had been captured, along with 2,500 tanks and 250 aircraft by Army Group Centre alone on their way to Moscow. The Red Army seemed on the verge of collapse.

The German advance was so fast, however, that supply lines were compromised and the German army had to pause. At this point Hitler intervened and ordered two of his most effective tank divisions north and south to support the other army groups. The sweep north and south was highly effective but had, however, one catastrophic effect as it delayed the journey east until after the arrival of winter. Whilst Red Army soldiers were equipped to deal with winter their German invaders were not.

Above: Two Wehrmacht soldiers are holding a Swastika flag to protect against friendly fire; fighting is going on nearby on the Eastern Front in Russia

Defending Moscow

The German Army Group Centre continued its push towards Moscow but suffered terribly through the Russian winter. Infantry soldiers were underfed and ill, and struggled to keep up with the rapidity of the Panzer advances. The Red Army in retreat also carried out a 'scorched earth' tactic where it destroyed or burned all equipment and supplies as it fled. They even poisoned the water rather than leave it to be used by the Germans. This left the Germans hungry and thirsty and lacking shelter.

By October 1942 Operation Typhoon, the main attempt to capture Moscow, was launched. Although some German soldiers reached the outskirts of Moscow they were ill equipped, and were driven back swiftly by General Zhukov with a loss of half a million soldiers. In spite of its initial successes, a lack of foresight and preparation for winter by the German military leadership left operation Barbarossa in tatters.

1941 Attack on Pearl Harbor

Pearl Harbor

Japan in the 1930s

Japan suffered badly in the Great Depression of the 1930s. In their anxiety to improve their lot the Japanese people had elected ever more militant and extreme governments until in the late 1930s they had a government who expressed sentiments of racial supremacy and a desire for colonial expansion. As an island, Japan was also short of natural resources and were looking for ways to fulfill this need. In 1931 Japan invaded Manchuria in northern China and rapidly exploited it with heavy industry. Fighting over the region continued and in 1937 Japan declared war on China.

The USA was wary of Japan's aggressive posturing and began to embargo trade on scrap iron and aviation fuel. This angered Japan and also drove it further towards desperate measures to obtain these materials.

'Neutral' USA

At the outbreak of World War Two, the USA was technically neutral although no one was in doubt about its real sympathies because it was using warships to escort British convoys and helping to produce arms for the Allied Forces. In 1940 Japan signed the Tripartite agreement with Italy and Germany. All three nations held views on racial supremacy and felt some political sympathy. The USA increased its trade embargoes against Japan still further as it didn't want, indirectly, to trade with Germany or Italy.

Japan was now desperate for supplies and planned to invade targets in South-East Asia such as the Philippines, Burma and Malaya. The only thing standing in the way of this invasion was the US Pacific fleet, based at Pearl Harbor.

Above: The front page of the
'New York World Telegram'

Above: USA warships on fire in Pearl Harbor

Below: The USS California on fire in Pearl Harbor

*Above: The American destroyer USS Shaw explodes
during the Japanese attack on Pearl Harbor*

Bombing begins

At 7.55am on 7th December 1941 the first wave of Japanese
bombers began to attack the US Pacific fleet which was
moored at Pearl Harbor on the Island of Oahu. Although the
US Government knew that war with Japan was imminent they
hadn't expected any attack to begin before the declaration of
war. US radar even picked up the bombers but thought they
were a fleet of B-17s coming in to land. Within two hours of
the attack beginning, five battleships had been sunk, another
sixteen damaged and 188 aircraft destroyed.

There were 2,400 American deaths with another 1,178
injuries. By chance three aircraft carriers which usually
moored at Pearl Harbor were elsewhere on the day, and
were unaffected by the attack.

A fatal error

The initial attack on Pearl Harbor was a success for the
Japanese. It bought them the vital time they needed to
occupy East India and by June 1942 they occupied territory
from Manchuria to the East Indies, and from the coast of
India deep into the Pacific.

Japan, however, had also hoped that the attack would
to some extent 'scare off' the Americans and in this they
fatally miscalculated. The American public was incensed
by the fact that Japan had attacked while the two nations
were still officially at peace and their indignation fortified
their determination to fight back in the years that followed.
The Americans quickly rebuilt their Pacific fleet to a higher
standard than before, and soon they were ready to fight
back with a vengeance.

1943 German Surrender at Stalingrad

Stalingrad

The battle for the Soviet Union

Despite their failure to capture Moscow in 1942, the Germans continued to make significant advances across the vast Russian front. In the North, German soldiers laid siege to Leningrad, the city named after Lenin who was the revolutionary founder of the communist Soviet Union. Victory to the South of the USSR was important too, where Hitler's objective was the oilfields of the Caucasus. Victory in the Caucasus would give Germany a huge strategic advantage.

As German armies A and B advanced south, however, Hitler was concerned about the city of Stalingrad. An important centre for communications and manufacturing base, it was also named after the Soviet leader, Joseph Stalin, who Hitler hated. To leave it in the hands of the Red Army as they advanced to the Caucasus would give the Soviets a chance to counter-attack from the rear, whilst defeating the leader's own namesake would strike a psychological blow for the Nazis.

Main: Battle of Stalingrad, fought between the German and Soviet army

Above: German commander of the 6th Army, Field Marshal Friedrich von Paulus, surrendering after his troops were besieged at Stalingrad

The attack begins

In September 1942 the leader of the German Sixth Army, von Paulus, began to advance on Stalingrad supported by the fourth Panzer division. Although severely damaged by operation Barbarossa, the Red Army knew they had to make a stand to defend the city that bore their leader's name. Stalin's order to his men was 'not a step back'.

In the initial advance, von Paulus laid siege to the city and eventually entered it to occupy some of the buildings. Resistance was bitter, however, with the Red Army defending their city brick by brick. Often, territory gained by the Germans by day was lost when the Soviets counter-attacked by night. By early November the temperature had dropped and the German army was short of warm clothes and adequate provisions.

Above: A view in 1943 of Stalingrad destroyed by German bombing

Von Paulus surrenders

On November 19th the Soviets were ready for a major counter attack. Marshal Zhukov, who had driven the Germans back at Moscow, now gathered seven army divisions close to Stalingrad. They encircled the city with one million men, trapping the Germans inside and cutting off all supplies from outside. Although von Paulus asked permission to retreat from Stalingrad as the encirclement started, Hitler would not allow it. In his communication to von Paulus he said, 'Surrender is forbidden. Sixth army will hold its position to the last man.'

By the end of February, starved and frozen, it was clear that the Sixth German Army was doomed. Against orders, von Paulus surrendered and 91,000 German soldiers were taken prisoner. Although Hitler was furious with the surrender, von Paulus possibly saved the lives of his remaining soldiers.

The God of war

It is a sobering thought that Europe owes its liberty to an army of peasant soldiers, scrabbling for life in a wrecked and tortured city. The Red Army in defence of their motherland proved invincible and Hitler's reckless determination not to surrender cost the Nazis not only countless lives but the loss of expertise and weaponry. With the Sixth Army vanquished the way was clear for a Soviet advance on Germany which the Nazis could do little to stop.

The Allies across Europe rejoiced at the victory in Stalingrad. At last here was a sign that Hitler and the forces of evil could be overturned. Hitler himself declared, 'The God of war has gone over to the other side.'

Main: German prisoners huddle with soldiers from other Axis satellite countries, against the sharp winds of the Russian winter

Main: American soldiers disembarking from an LCI landing craft upon its arrival on the beaches of Normandy for Operation Overlord

1944 The D-Day Landings turn the tide of war

D-Day

Above: Royal Navy Commandos of the Landing Craft Obstacle Clearance Units running to get clear

A Second Front

After the Allies were driven from Dunkirk in 1940 it became apparent that pushing the Germans back out of France and the rest of Western Europe would be no easy task. The Germans had fortified the coast heavily at the points where it was closest to Britain and they had established control in towns and cities right across Europe. In 1941 Stalin began calls for a second front to be opened in the West, to relieve pressure on the USSR and Eastern Europe.

The Allied forces, now including America, began to formulate a plan and Lieutenant General F.E. Morgan was given the task of identifying the best location to begin an invasion. Eventually he settled on the beaches at Normandy. They were not as heavily fortified as other possible sites, and the Navy would be able to make use of the ports of Southampton, Portsmouth and Poole.

Operation Overlord

The codename given to the D-Day landings was Operation Overlord. By 1943 the command structure was in place and included a wealth of successful and experienced commanders. Dwight Eisenhower was made supreme commander of the invasion force and Air Chief-Marshal Arthur Tedder was made his deputy. Two army groups were created, an American one under General Omar Bradley, and a British one under Bernard Montgomery. Montgomery was also given command of all land forces during the assault phase of the attack.

The invasion was scheduled for May 1944 but as the day approached it became clear that a larger landing force would be required and therefore more landing vessels. The date was pushed back to June 6th to allow for more landing vessels to be built.

Above: D-Day, 6th June 1944, is still one of the world's most consequential battles, as the Allied landing in Normandy led to the liberation of France which marked a turning point in World War Two

Above: US soldiers gather around trucks disembarking from landing crafts shortly after D-Day 6th June 1944

D-Day

Five beaches were the initial focus of the invasion. Two beaches, codenamed Utah and Omaha would be for the Americans, two more, Gold and Sword, for the British and one, Juno, for the Canadians. Operation Neptune was the name given to the operation to cross the Channel, which involved 6,000 boats including battleships, tugs, landing vessels and supply ships. There were even two 'portable' harbours or Mulberry Harbours. When constructed, these floating piers could be used to land 7,000 tons of vehicles and equipment in a day.

There was little resistance at the beaches themselves except at Omaha where American soldiers had to scale cliffs under heavy gunfire. The Americans moved west towards Brittany whilst the British and Canadians moved inland towards Caen. Here the Allies fought bitterly to drive out the Germans, who defended Normandy with heavy artillery and 'Tiger' Tanks. Although the Tiger and King Tiger Tanks had greater firepower than the British Shermans, they ran out of fuel quickly which was to prove a major Achilles heel.

Allied success

The Germans knew that their position would be weaker the further the Allies advanced into France. For that reason, control of Normandy was vital. The Germans fought hard to hold the city of Caen, but after heavy bombing this eventually fell to the Allies. Progress for the Allies was slow but by August of 1944 they succeeded in surrounding and capturing 150,000 German soldiers at the town of Falaise and this effectively constituted the end of the battle in Normandy and the start of the German retreat in Western Europe.

D-Day was the largest and most complicated invasion ever seen, its genius being seen not only in the fighting but in the planning and provisioning that supported the soldiers. For the Germans in the West it really was the beginning of the end.

Main: US troops march up beachhead while landing craft in rear continue to unload supplies

1945 The Atom Bomb is Dropped

Atom Bomb

World War Two in the East

From 1942 Japan occupied huge areas of the Far East in order to maintain its supply of minerals, oil and food. At the beginning of 1945 Germany was all-but defeated and so Japan had lost its greatest ally, but in spite of the vast superiority of American resources and military might, Japan would not agree to an unconditional surrender and fought with a ferocity like no other nation.

The USA originally believed that Japan would have to be beaten by means of an invasion. To achieve this they estimated the needed a force of around one million troops, around a quarter of whom they expected to lose. For this reason Harry Truman, who was sworn in as president in 1945, came to believe that dropping the atom bomb on selected targets would be the most effective way to end the war quickly and with the smallest loss of life.

The Manhattan project

Research on the atom bomb had been underway for some time. In 1942 two Hungarian refugees from Nazi Germany Leo Szilard and Eurene Wigner became convinced that Germany was developing an atom bomb. They were so concerned that they wrote to Albert Einstein, and Einstein in turn wrote to President Roosevelt. The purpose of this letter was to suggest that the USA should also arm itself with an atom bomb in order to defend itself should Germany succeed. Unknown to the Allies, Germany abandoned its atom bomb project in 1942 following an assault on its specialist labouratory in Norway and never re-started, believing it did not need an atom bomb to win the war.

The Americans, however, persevered with their experiments, pouring millions of dollars into the development of this most terrible weapon. The experimental work to produce an atom bomb was called the Manhattan project.

Above: Captain William Parsons, the Naval Ordnance expert, who helped with the making of the atomic bomb

Main: Hiroshima after the atom bomb of 6th August, 1945

Above: Little Boy in the bomb pit

Enola Gay

On 26th July 1945 the Allies met in Potsdam to discuss the European treaty, and also to demand an unconditional surrender from the Japanese. On July 28th the Japanese refused. On the way home from the conference, Truman gave the order that they should prepare to drop the atom bomb. Possible targets were discussed. Among the list of possible towns were Hiroshima and Nagasaki, both were manufacturing centres, and Hiroshima had an army base.

The first target to be selected was Hiroshima. On 6th August 1945 the order came through that the Enola Gay, a B-29 superfortress based in Tinian, was to take the atom bomb, nicknamed 'Little Boy' and drop it on the town.

Devastation

The bomb was released at 8.16am. It floated down with a parachute and exploded in the air at around 2,000 feet. 60-80,000 people died instantly, some simply vanishing in the intense heat. Many more thousands died in the following months from burns or radiation sickness. Just two days later the US dropped a second bomb on Nagasaki with the loss of a further 50,000 lives.

Robert Lewis, co-pilot on the Enola Gay, recorded this: 'I honestly have the feeling of groping for words to explain this or I might say, "my God what have we done?"'

The Japanese President, Hirohito, surrendered. There is still fierce debate about whether the US was justified in dropping the atom bomb but the terrible images from Hiroshima have haunted the minds and souls of those that have seen them. The name Hiroshima sounds a warning through the years against the use of ultimate force. It is a terrible reminder of man's destructive power.

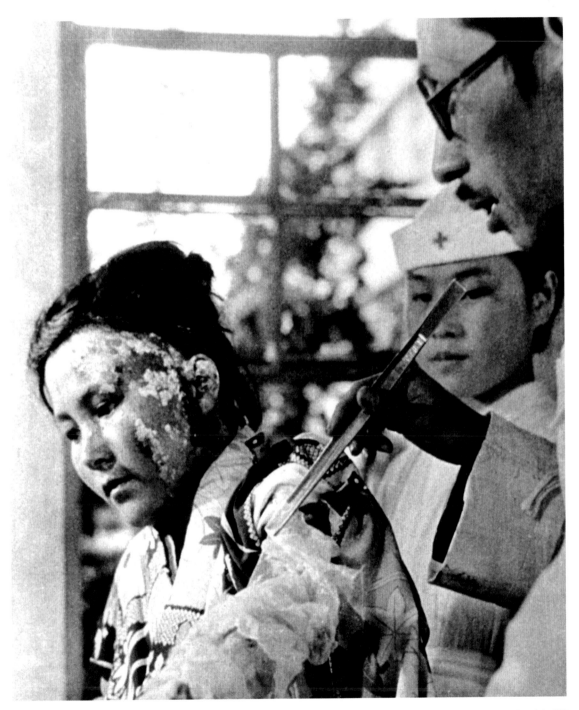

Above: Hiroshima bombing victim, 1945

Main: The second
American atom
bomb launched on
Japan exploded over
the city of Nagasaki

1947 The Partition of India

India

The British in India

The British had maintained a presence in India since the 1600s with the development of the East India Company, but it was not until 1858 that the British officially assumed control of the Indian Government. India was an attractive conquest, boasting a rich variety of cash crops such as cotton and tea. Ruled as it was in provinces by many royal families, the British succeeded in governing India by flattering and supporting wealthy Indian families who in turn kept ordinary working Indians in their place.

There was resistance to British rule, however, and this grew stronger with each passing year. The Indian National Congress was formed in 1885, initially to unite all Indians and strengthen bonds with the British, but it quickly became a rallying point for the Home Rule movement, especially under the leadership of Gandhi from the 1920s onwards.

Above: At the New Delhi conference on the partition of India are (left to right) Communications Member Sardar Abdur Rab Nishtar; Defence Member Sardar Baldev Singh; President of the Indian National Congress Acharya J B Kripalani; Home and Information and Broadcasting Member Vallabhai Patel; Advisor to the Viceroy Sir Eric Melville; Vice-President of the Interim Government Pandit Jawaharlal Nehru; Lord Mountbatten; and Finance Member Liaquat Ali Khan

Main: A delegation of Sikhs leaving Downing Street, London, after presenting a petition calling for the whole of the Punjab region to be included in the state of India, rather than Pakistan

Hindus and Muslims

Although united in its opposition to British rule, India was not united within itself. For years, a simmering power struggle had existed between Hindus and Muslims. Muslims, the former rulers of India under the Mughal Empire, felt that Hindus as the present rulers of India were given too many unfair privileges by the British. Hindus occupied the best government positions and in schools, children were made to sing the Hindu anthem which contained anti-Muslim sentiments.

In 1906 the Muslim League was formed to promote Muslim interests within India. Some within the League called for a separate Muslim state to be formed as well as an independent India. The British ignored both requests. With the start of World War Two, however, the Indian National Congress refused to participate in fighting whereas the Muslim League supported the British war effort. This made the British more sympathetic to their aims.

The partition

In 1945 Britain's economy was left in ruins by World War Two and the new Labour government felt that governing India was an expense and a strain they could do without. Negotiations began between Viceroy Lord Louis Mountbatten and the two largest representative parties, the Indian National Congress led by Jawaharlal Nehru and the Muslim League led by Mohammed Ali Jinnah. The resulting plan was two separate Muslim states, East and West Pakistan to either side of India, and a free state of India which was to be run by a Hindu majority.

In 1947, Pakistan announced its independence as a new state on 14th of August, followed by India on 15th August. The hurriedly-drawn border was announced on 17th April. Based on outdated maps, it cut states, towns, villages and even families in half.

Independent states

The period after the partition left terrible confusion and perhaps millions of deaths. It brought about the largest mass migration of people ever seen with some 15 million people moving state. The area of Kashmir which lay on the border was claimed by both sides and remains a source of conflict today. Some of the decisions regarding the border just didn't make sense, for example the majority of support for the Muslim League came from Uttar Pradesh, which was not included in Pakistan. Furthermore, much of the population was tied by family and history to certain areas rather than by religion which made them reluctant to move.

Perhaps the most long-term problem was the difference in wealth afforded to each country. The new India contained 90% of the industrial capability of the old India. The division of wealth was also unequal with the new state of Pakistan receiving only 17% of British India's reserves. This left Pakistan very much as India's poor cousin, a source of persistent conflict.

Above: One of 30 special trains leaving New Delhi Station which took the staff of the Pakistani government to Karachi

Main: Muslim refugees from India at a refugee camp, 1947

1947 The First Faster-than-sound Flight

Supersonic Flight

Flight takes off

From its first shaky start with the Wright Brothers in 1903, flight technology advanced rapidly. This was partly owing to the frantic innovation surrounding two World Wars. Having established the potential of the plane for fast travel, scientists and engineers were now intrigued to see how fast planes could actually be made to go.

In 1945 a British fighter plane called the Gloster Meteor set a new world record for speed at 606.25 miles per hour – not far below the speed of sound. There had been unofficial reports of planes breaking the sound barrier in World War Two during evasive dives, but these were unconfirmed. The race was on to develop a plane capable of travelling at Mach-1.

Mach - 1

Mach -1, named after 19th Century German physicist Ernst Mach, is the name given to the speed at which sound travels. Sound travels at different speeds depending on altitude. At sea level the speed of sound is 761mph whereas at 20,000 feet in altitude it is 660 feet.

The plane that designed to fly at this speed was called the Bell X-1. It was shaped like a .50 calibre bullet to make it aerodynamic and it had thin but extremely strong wings. It also had a horizontal stabilizer which could be turned up and down to provide extra stability at high speeds. It had a wingspan of 8.5 metres and a length of 9.4 metres. The X-1 carried more than 230kg of flight test instruments.

Above: Charles E. Yeager showing a model of the Bell-X 1

Main: Captain Charles Yeager, Major Gus Lundquist and Captain James Fitzgerald standing in front of a Bell X-1

Main: Charles E. Yeager steps out of a plane at Edwards Air Force Base in California to be congratulated by Lawrence D. Bell, president of Bell Aircraft Corporation

Glamorous Glennis

The pilot chosen to fly the Bell X-1 was Charles 'Chuck' Yeager, and he named the plane Glamorous Glennis after his wife. Yeager had been an ace fighter pilot in World War Two and since the war had made a living as a test pilot. Two days before his attempt to fly at the speed of sound he broke two of his ribs in a riding accident and was in terrible pain on the day of the test.

On 14th October 1947, the Glamorous Glennis was taken up in the bomb hold of a B-29 superfortress and air-launched at an altitude of 7,000 metres. Using his rocket to climb to a height of 43,000 feet, Yeager flew the plane at Mach 1.06 or 700mph. In subsequent flights Yeager increased this to 957mph.

Supersonic

Yeager went on to test further experimental aircraft for the US Air Force, until he was appointed Director of the Space School, later to become NASA. Here he trained astronauts for take-off.

Since Yeager first broke the sound barrier in 1947 planes have travelled faster and faster. It is not only fighter planes and space rockets that make use of great speed either. Concorde, the World's first supersonic passenger aircraft commissioned in the 1970s, came to be seen as the most glamorous way to travel. Yeager's unique combination of skill and daring ushered in a new age of speed, enabling space travel and bringing new ways to cross the World's ever-shrinking distances.

Above: The Bell-X 1

1948 The State of Israel is Proclaimed

Israel

Before 1948

Between 1920 and 1948 the area known as Palestine in the Middle East was home to Arabs who had lived there under Ottoman rule, and many new Jewish settlers. The Jewish settlers believed that the British, among others, had promised them an area of Palestine under the Balfour Declaration and hoped to claim it, believing it to be the 'Promised Land' of the Old Testament. The Arab Palestinians also believed they had been promised the land in return for supporting the Allies in World War One.

By 1929 the Jewish population in Palestine was growing rapidly, especially in Jerusalem which was a city of religious significance for both Arabs and Jews. The creation of a Jewish Agency to promote Jewish interests in Palestine made the Arabs anxious. They felt that the Jewish population was using it to promote their interests above those of the Arabs in order to form their own state.

The new state of Israel

In May 1948 The Jewish Agency declared an independent state of Israel on land that had formerly been Palestine. The United Nations, along with some western nations, were quick to recognize the legitimacy of the state, although the Palestinians and other Arab neighbours in the region did not accept it and attacked Israel. The new Prime Minister, David Ben Gurion used a surprisingly formidable and well equipped army to establish and defend Israel.

The proclamation of the State of Israel is still a controversial subject for many people who believe that the Palestinians were treated unfairly. Israelis, however, believe that they have a religious justification for living in Jerusalem. Today, Israel has expanded to occupy more land previously occupied by Palestinians and constant friction between the two groups is a source of tension in the Middle East.

Below: The crowd of Jews assembled in the streets of Tel Aviv 20th May
1948 a few hours before the British Mandate in Palestine ended

Above: The first Israeli Prime minister David
Ben-Gurion (standing)

Above: A line of people watch as a supply plane arrives to deliver food and other staples during the Berlin Airlift after World War Two

1948 The Berlin Blockade Begins

Berlin

The aftermath of World War Two

At the end of World War Two Europe was in chaos. Germany had no stable government and had been crushed morally and economically by defeat. Britain, France and the USSR, as the remaining dominant nations within Europe, also set about starting to rebuild themselves after heavy losses. Lessons had been learned from World War One, however, that crushing a country like Germany would only make it thirst for revenge so the Allies planned to rebuild Germany as they themselves became stronger.

In the immediate aftermath of war, Germany was governed in four zones, a British zone, a French zone, an American zone and a Soviet zone. Berlin fell within the Soviet zone but itself was also divided into four zones.

Relations with the USSR

Britain, France and the USA had always mistrusted the USSR under Stalin, even though they fought on the same side in World War Two. The USSR had been communist since 1920 and communism was widely mistrusted throughout the rest of Europe. Also, the USSR had suffered heavily in World War Two and was eager to protect its own interests by occupying as many countries as possible to make use of their resources. It took huge reparations from the Soviet zone of Germany.

Throughout 1947 and 1948 the USA, Britain and France discussed the future for Germany but the USSR played no part. In the Soviet zone, western literature was banned while the Soviets distributed anti-western propaganda. Then in June 1948 Britain, France and the USA announced that they wanted to combine their three zones in one West German state. This was followed on June 23rd by the introduction of a new currency to improve German trade.

*Above: An East German passes by a placard
announcing 'You are now leaving British sector'*

Above: Boxes of pineapple and sacks of flour stacked up in a West Berlin warehouse during the Berlin Airlift in case of another Berlin blockade

The blockade begins

The day after the introduction of the new currency for West Germany was chaos in the Soviet zone of Berlin as people tried to get rid of their old currency and buy the new one. Soviet leader Stalin felt threatened by the new country of West Germany and feared that those in the Soviet zone would try to leave. He began a blockade of Berlin, cutting off all the roads into the new West German zone.

The British, Americans and French believed that Stalin was trying to starve the population into joining together with the Soviet zone. The Allies decided they would have to supply Berlin by air, and over the 318 days of the blockade flew in 275,000 planes of food and supplies. A supply plane landed every three minutes at Berlin's Templehof airport.

Above: A worker carries supplies from a British aircraft during the Berlin Airlift

The Iron Curtain comes down

On 12th May Stalin called off the blockade but the incident had set the tone of East-West relations for many years to come. It showed clearly that Stalin was hungry for territory and eager to spread the influence of communism. The Berlin Wall, a potent symbol of the Iron Curtain that existed across Eastern Europe, was built to separate communist East Berlin from capitalist West Berlin and stayed there until 1989 by which time families and friends had been separated on opposite sides of the wall for decades.

Not Germany but the USSR was now the enemy for USA, Britain and France and the Cold War began, with both sides building more and deadlier weapons. In 1949 the North Atlantic Treaty Organization (NATO) was set up to defend its signatories against the threat of communism. An enmity which would define much of the 20th Century had begun in earnest.

1948 Universal Declaration of Human Rights Adopted

Human Rights

A post-war world

I n the years that followed World War Two, more and more was discovered about atrocities committed by different countries. The worst of these atrocities was the Nazi Holocaust, an evil regime whereby German citizens of Jewish descent and Jews born in the countries occupied by Germany, were rounded up and sent to concentration camps. Many were then exterminated or forced to live in intolerable conditions purely because of their religion or ethnicity. The Nazis treated other groups like this too, such as Eastern Europeans and the disabled.

World leaders were appalled by the fact that such cruelty had been allowed to happen and they wanted to find a way to stop it happening again. In 1946 the newly created United Nations set up a Commission on Human Rights to find out how this could be achieved.

Above: One of the first documents published by the United Nations, The Universal Declaration of Human Rights

Main: 10th December, 1948, the Universal Declaration of
Human Rights was adopted at the Palais de Chaillot in Paris

The Commission on Human Rights

The United Nations was established in 1945 to provide a platform on which representatives from different countries could meet and discuss their differences and make plans together. There were 56 original members, and neither Germany nor Japan was initially included. The initial charter of the United Nations 'reaffirmed faith in fundamental human rights, and dignity and worth of the human person'. But it was quickly realized that this charter did not sufficiently clarify what constituted the correct observance of human rights.

For this reason the Commission on Human Rights was established. One of the basic tasks of the Commission was to establish what constituted reasonable human rights. It was clear that making this decision could no longer be left to individual governments to decide, as some countries were guilty of mistreating their own citizens.

The Universal Declaration of Human Rights

Finally the Commission defined thirty guiding articles which were adopted in 1948. The articles covered abuses of human rights such as torture, slavery, persecution and injustice regarding gender, religion or ethnicity. The first article is a summation of the whole purpose of the declaration.

'All human beings are born equal in dignity and rights. They are endowed with reason and conscience and should act towards one another in a spirit of brotherhood.'

Forty-eight nations signed the declaration but there were eight abstentions from eastern bloc countries, South Africa and Saudi Arabia. The eastern bloc countries had some disagreements over wording which concerned ownership of property and economic freedom. In the years following the declaration a second alternative version was drawn up in which the Soviet bloc signed in 1966.

Main: The Eiffel Tower with the flags of the countries participating in the United Nations General Assembly

Human rights in the world

Since 1948 the UN has grown to include 193 members and human rights are championed around the world. The UN continues its work through many agencies and committees such as the United Nations International Children's Emergency Fund, the World Food Program and many others. The UN can supply soldiers, medics and reconstruction workers to disaster zones and can send a single representative to speak for most of the World.

Whilst human rights abuses are unfortunately still widespread it is possible to identify these abuses and apply pressure to those who carry them out. The Universal Declaration for Human Rights recognized the precious nature of human life and is a turning point for the way all people are treated.

Above: Eleanor Roosevelt at a conference for human rights

1949 Hubble First Uses the Hale Telescope

The Telescope

Edwin Hubble

E dwin Hubble is considered by many to be the father of observational cosmology. Born in 1889, he began his studies as a law student and set up his own legal practice, but it quickly became clear that his real passion was for astronomy, so Hubble returned to University in Chicago where he received a doctorate in astronomy. In 1919 he was given a staff position by George Ellery Hale at the Mount Wilson Observatory in Pasadena, California where he worked until his death.

Hubble is perhaps most notable for 'Hubble's Law'. 'Hubble's Law' proved that the universe is expanding. Albert Einstein visited Hubble at his observatory in Mount Wilson to congratulate him for this discovery although it disproved Einstein's earlier theory that the universe was of constant size.

Beyond the Milky Way

In 1922 astronomers believed that the Milky Way Galaxy constituted the entire universe. Hubble made a study of faint nebulae using the Hooker telescope at the Mount Wilson Observatory and identified several Cepheid Variables (a type of star) in several spiral nebulae including the Andromeda Nebula. His observations about these proved that they were too distant to be part of the Milky Way but were part of other galaxies outside our own.

Many scientists scoffed at these discoveries as they challenged the astronomical world's entire understanding of the universe, but Hubble had his theories published in the New York Times and on January 1st 1925 presented his theories to the Astronomical Association. He was later given an award of $500 and had his work published.

Above: A portrait of Hubble from 1948

Above: Hubble was the first scientist to offer observational evidence supporting the theory, now known as Hubble's Law, of the expansion of the universe

The Hale telescope

Named after George Ellery Hale, a noted astrophysicist who worked tirelessly on the building of new telescopes, the Hale telescope was one of the most remarkable engineering feats of the 20th century. Hale wanted to build a telescope with a mirror measuring 200 inches, or twice the diameter of the largest existing reflector. The main problem in creating this telescope was in casting the glass mirror as glass was inclined to expand and contract with heat and would cause imperfections in images.

Ellery began to experiment with Pyrex and after a great deal of testing, grinding and polishing, a flawless reflector was achieved. The production of the reflector was interrupted by World War Two and sadly Hale did not live to see the masterpiece that bears his name.

A whole new universe

The Hale telescope provided a view of the universe that astronomers had only dreamed of. It couldn't only show how far away objects in space were but what they looked like and how they behaved. Using Hale, Walter Baade measured the distance to Andromeda to be two billion light years, thus doubling the size of the known universe, and Walter Sandage discovered quasars which were billions of years old. Astronomers began to understand how the universe had formed and to learn how old the stars were.

Hubble died shortly after the Hale telescope was completed but through his final planning and design of the Hale telescope he finally got a closer look at the new galaxies he had discovered and paved the way for a millennia of new space discoveries.

Above: Albert Einstein visiting Mount Wilson Observatory, California

1950 The Battle of Inchon

Korean War

The 38th parallel

At the close of World War Two, Korea was promised the opportunity to become an independent state, free from Japan. As Japan surrendered, General Douglas MacArthur formulated a plan that called for the creation of an artificial line or border along the 38th parallel. The area north of the border, called North Korea, would surrender to the Soviets and the area to the south, South Korea, would surrender to the Americans.

In the years following the war, America supported a capitalist government under new President, Syngman Rhee in the south. It was intended that North and South Korea would unite after five years, but North Korea under Kim Il Sung remained in the hands of Communists while South Korea became democratic.

Above: American troops climbing down guide nets into assault craft in preparation for the first great counter-strike of the Korean campaign

North Korea invades

In June 1950 communist North Korea invaded the south. The initial attack was a stunning success and UN troops present in South Korea were pushed back to an area on the peninsula known as the Pusan Perimetre. The newly created UN Security Council considered this to be an act of war. General MacArthur suggested a daring strike on the west coast at Inchon. Many were sceptical about these plans as the approach to Inchon was narrow and easily defended, but MacArthur argued that its unlikeliness as a suitable place for invasion would provide an advantage.

A joint CIA-military operation led by Navy Lieutenant Eugene Clark landed on Yonghung-Do Island a week before the planned invasion. They provided vital intelligence to support the US-led troops.

The Inchon Landings

On 15th September 1950 the UN fleet, consisting mainly of US military, and aging equipment salvaged from World War Two, moved into position around Inchon. Battleships had previously been shelling NKPA (North Korean People's Army) positions around Wolmi-Do Island. In spite of this significant warning of impending invasion the NKPA commander at Wolmi-Do assured NKPA command that he could repel any attack.

At 6.30am the 5th marines came ashore at Green Beach and secured Wolmi-do Island. They were followed by 1st marines at Red Beach later in the afternoon. The UN troops headed by the marines secured the causeway and captured Inchon with few casualties. As further UN troops landed at Inchon, the trapped UN troops at the Pusan Perimetre also broke free and pushed the NKPA back to Seoul. Fighting was fierce for the capital but Seoul was finally taken from the NKPA on 25th September.

Conflicting ideologies

The Inchon landings were the first skirmish in a war of ideologies between North and South Korea. Fighting continued for several years and was only ended with a fragile truce, though not a long-term solution, in 1953. Now not only divided by the 38th parallel but by a different way of life and conflicting politics, the people of North and South Korea remain separate to this day.

The war in Korea was also the first sign of a much broader global conflict of ideology with the massive communist states of the USSR and China on one side and the Capitalist West on the other. The USSR and China had supported the North Korean government while the people of Seoul looked to the West. It was another small step on the way to the extreme hostilities of the Cold War.

Above: US Marines in amphibious assault craft moving towards Inchon in the first counter-attack of the Korean War

Main: American soldiers push inland from Inchon, 1950

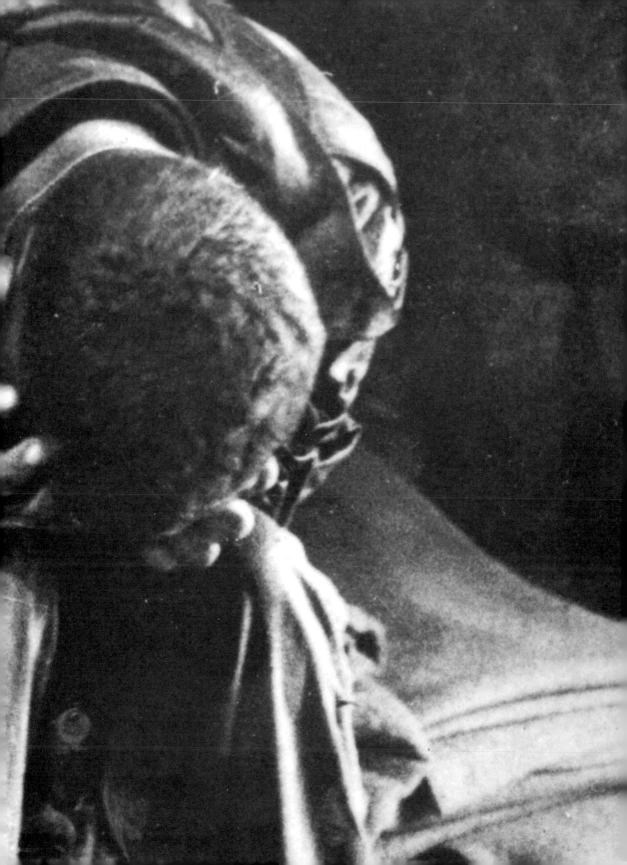

1953 The Discovery of the Structure of DNA

DNA

The same eyes

It has always been accepted that children inherit physical and behavioural characteristics from their parents, but it was not until the 20th Century that scientists really began to understand how inherited characteristics were passed on biologically. In 1868 Deoxyribonucleic acid (DNA) was discovered by a Swiss Medical Student called Johann Friedrich Miescher while he was working on white blood cells, but it was not recognized as genetic material for another 50 years.

In 1953 Scientists James Watson and Francis Crick, using research by Rosalind Franklin, discovered that DNA contained the genetic code for all living things. It showed how genetic material was passed from one person to another.

What is DNA?

DNA stores genetic information and passes it onto the next generation. When reproduction occurs, a copy of the 'parent' DNA is made and a copy is passed to the offspring. The information in the cell then forms the physical characteristics of the new body. DNA is divided into strands called chromosomes, or genes. Genes determine the way particular characteristics show themselves.

Within a DNA molecule there are also four nitrogen-rich bases. These are adenine, guanine, thymine and cytosine. Combined with deoxyribrose and phosphate molecules, these are the building blocks of nucleotides and nucleotides are the building blocks of DNA. Nucleotides form pairs and join together to make a double helix.

Above: Dr Francis Harry Compton Crick, co-winner of the 1962 Nobel prize for medicine

Above: Sir William Lawrence Bragg headed the Cavendish Labouratory in Cambridge supporting James Watson and Francis Crick in their pioneering work, deducing the helical structure of DNA using X-ray crystal studies

The human genome

Each organism has a set of chromosomes that contain all of its genetic information. The human genome is made of 46 chromosomes found in the nucleus of each cell. The chromosomes are organized into 23 pairs – one chromosome of each pair is inherited from the mother and one from the father. One pair of chromosomes, X and Y, determines gender.

Carried among these molecules are 35,000 genes, each of which determines an individual characteristic. The Human Genome Project is to determine the entire sequence of each DNA molecule and the location and identity of the genes. In June 2000 a 'working draft' DNA sequence of the human genome was completed.

The riddle of life

For most people, understanding more about the structure of DNA and the human genome is a good thing. It leads to a greater understanding of disease or inherited conditions such as heart trouble. Some genes have found to be markers for specific diseases like cancer. It is also used to prove connections between family members or ancient ancestors. It is now possible to take a test to prove paternity of a child, and some people have started to trace connections between their own DNA and that of ancestors from centuries before.

There is also concern, however, that the ability to control human genetics could create problems of an ethical nature. Parents could select the genetic code of their future offspring to ensure not only freedom from illness but also intelligence, ability or gender. Individuals with a gene likely to produce illnesses or certain behavioural traits could become targets for discrimination.

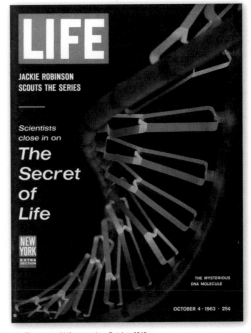

Above: The cover of Life magazine, October 1963

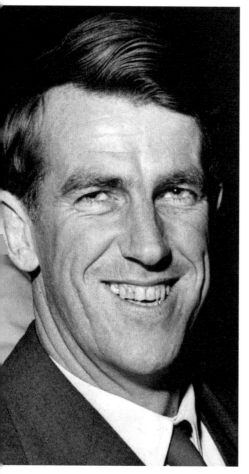

Above: Sir Edmund Hillary

1953 The Conquest of Everest

Mount Everest

The Highest Peak

For climbers and mountaineers in the first half of the 20th Century, the summit of Mount Everest in the Himalayas was the most appealing, yet the most elusive conquest of all. At 29,028 feet it claimed the lives of one British expedition in 1924. George Mallory and Andrew Irvine may have been seen less than 800 feet from the summit, and there is some speculation as to whether they reached it, but they never returned to their camp so whether they succeeded or failed is unknown. Attempts at the summit of Everest were made by mountaineering parties from other countries but it was not until 1953 that anyone succeeded in achieving this ultimate feat.

Everest was named after Sir George Everest, the surveyor who was the first person to produce maps of the subcontinent of India including the Himalayas.

Edmund Hillary and Tenzing Norgay

In 1953, the ninth British Everest expedition was launched, led by Colonel John Hunt. New Zealander Edmund Hillary and Tenzing Norgay were two of the team, and both had formed part of previous successful exploratory parties to the Himalayas. Hillary had been a pilot during World War Two and had been involved in many climbing expeditions after the war. In 1951 he had formed part of a team led by Eric Shipton which had discovered the southern route to the peak. This was the route via which the successful ascent would be made.

Tenzing Norgay, whose exact age at the time of the Hunt expedition was not known, was a Sherpa, who had begun his mountaineering career as a guide but following fantastic climbing performances and a rescue of one of his comrades in a Swiss expedition, he was given a full role in the climbing team.

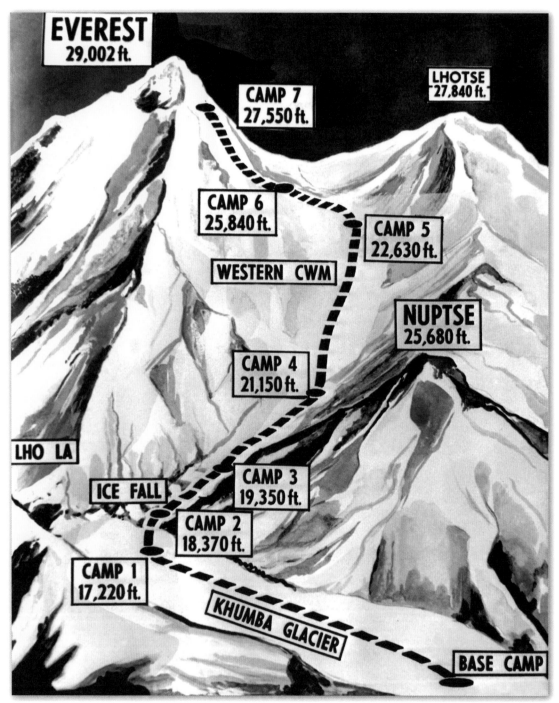

EVEREST
29,002 ft.

LHOTSE
27,840 ft.

CAMP 7
27,550 ft.

CAMP 6
25,840 ft.

CAMP 5
22,630 ft.

WESTERN CWM

NUPTSE
25,680 ft.

CAMP 4
21,150 ft.

LHO LA

ICE FALL

CAMP 3
19,350 ft.

CAMP 2
18,370 ft.

CAMP 1
17,220 ft.

KHUMBA GLACIER

BASE CAMP

Above: Hillary's Expedition itinerary in 1953

Reaching the summit

Colonel Hunt's expedition involved more than 400 people including 362 porters and 20 Sherpa guides. The team got to base camp in March and slowly moved camps up the mountain until their final camp at the South Col was built at 25,900 feet. During preparations for the push to the summit, Hillary had a near miss when he fell down a crevasse but was saved by the quick actions of Tenzing. He then wanted Tenzing to be his partner in the final climb.

Hillary and Tenzing set out on 28th May. On the morning of the 29th Hillary spent two hours defrosting his boots before setting off. Following a 40 foot rock climb with 30lb packs the two reached the summit at 11.30 but owing to the harsh conditions they only stayed at the top for 15 minutes.

The ultimate achievement

When Hillary and Tenzing came down the mountain, their team at the South Col camp first thought that they had failed because of their exhausted demeanour, but when the successful duo were 100 metres away they began to wave and point and wild celebrations ensued. A journalist from the London Times and another mountaineer hurried as fast as they could back to Kathmandu, so that they could get the news of Everest's conquest over to Britain by 2nd June, the coronation of Queen Elizabeth II.

When the whole team reached Kathmandu they were mobbed by locals. Colonel Hunt and Edmund Hillary were immediately knighted and Tenzing Norgay was later awarded the George Cross. The conquest of Everest in the optimistic, forward-looking 1950s was seen as a further sign of man's increasing mastery over science, nature and the Earth itself.

Above: The victorious Mount Everest climbing team arrive at London Airport

**1954 Edward Murrow Attacks
Senator Joseph McCarthy**

Communism

The Red Threat

In the early 1950s the communists in Eastern Europe and the Far East appeared to be flourishing. The USSR had taken over control of a number of satellite countries like Czechoslovakia and Yugoslavia which it kept behind the Iron Curtain and indoctrinated with communist ideology. China, another country of giant proportions, was also pursuing communist ideology with disregard for other beliefs and freedom of expression. The sudden and aggressive development of global communism led to an acute rivalry and paranoia between the capitalist West and the communist East.

In the USA anyone suspected of communist sympathies was considered unpatriotic and many famous Hollywood names suspected of communism were questioned by the House of Un-American Activities Committee. Suspicion was rife, and many who had previously been communists named names in order to avoid prison.

Joseph McCarthy

Born in 1908, Joseph McCarthy first trained as a lawyer. When the USA entered the Second World War, McCarthy enlisted to serve in the US Marines where he took part in training exercises but was mainly employed on clerical duties. At the end of the war, he decided to run for the Senate as a Republican candidate in Wisconsin against Robert La Florette. His campaign was notable for smears about the age and war record of his opponent whom he claimed had made profit out of the war. In the end, owing to his devious tactics, McCarthy won a place in the Senate by a narrow majority.

McCarthy's performance in the Senate was unremarkable, and by 1950 he was being investigated for tax fraud and bribe-taking. Afraid he would not be re-elected, he asked advice from his friend Edmund Walsh. Walsh, a priest, suggested that McCarthy should raise his profile by hunting out suspected communists working for the Democrats.

Above: Joseph McCarthy during an interview on the news program 'See It Now,' 9th March, 1954

Main: American news commentator and broadcast journalist Edward R. Murrow

*Main: Edward R. Murrow (L) and Fred W. Friendly (R) who in
1954 used the CBS News television broadcast 'See it Now' to
expose the powerful Senator Joseph McCarthy*

Anti-communist hysteria

On 9th February 1950 McCarthy made a speech where he claimed to have a list of 205 people in the State Department that were members of the American Communist Party. He also received information about suspected communists working within the government from his friend in the FBI, J. Edgar Hoover. With this, McCarthy began a witch-hunt. McCarthy's actions raised anti-communist feeling to hysterical levels and the practice of hunting out communists became known as McCarthyism. People went in fear of what others would report about them whether fairly or unfairly. An accusation from McCarthy, however unfounded, could end anyone's career.

Not everyone, however, agreed with the brutal approach that McCarthy took and ultimately President Dwight Eisenhower himself became critical of McCarthy's methods. The press sensed that the tide of public opinion was changing and criticism of him began to appear in the papers.

Edward Murrow

On the 9th of March 1954, Edward Murrow, one of the most respected journalists in the USA, decided to devote his 'See It Now' programme to an attack on McCarthyism. His criticism arose from his belief that the USA should be a free nation in which people should be free to express their views without fear, and to associate with whichever friends they pleased. He declared, 'We will not be driven by fear into an age of unreason.'. The programme received massive endorsement from the American public. It was a defining moment for the USA who, as a nation, decided that plurality and freedom were preferable to a reign of terror which brought them to the same level as the communist nations they feared.

Having lost public and government support, McCarthy's career soon ended and he died later as the result of alcoholism.

Above: Edward R. Murrow as he delivers an investigative report

*Above: Inventor of the polio
vaccine Dr. Jonas E. Salk*

1955: Successful Polio Vaccine
Announced to the World

Polio

Polio epidemics

In the post-war years polio was one of the biggest killers of children in the developed world. The initial symptoms were flu-like and highly infections, spreading most quickly in the summer. Certain years saw serious epidemics develop when families had to be quarantined until the infection passed. In 1952 the USA had one of its worst epidemics when more than 58,000 people contracted the disease. More than three thousand of these died and a further 21,000 were left with permanent physical disability as a result.

The consequences of the disease were so severe that it was regarded almost as a modern plague and fear of polio was extreme. In times of severe epidemic, parents kept their children out of school and away from public places.

Jonas Salk

Born on October 28th 1914 to Irish Jewish immigrant parents, Jonas Salk was a committed and able student from the outset. At the age of 13 he entered the Townsend Harris High School, a publicly funded school for gifted children whose parents could not otherwise have afforded a good education. From there he went to City College New York, a well-regarded university with no tuition fees, to study medicine. Fellow students remembered him as a voracious reader. He was also notable among his peers as he had no intention of working as a practising doctor. He favoured a career in medical research where he would be able to help mankind in general. To this end he studied biochemistry and bacteriology as well as medicine.

On leaving university he was offered a job researching the influenza virus, and from there went on to secure his own lab at the University of Pittsburgh School of Medicine.

Main: An operative in the Glaxo Laboratories mixes three distinct strains of killed polio virus to prepare the final vaccine

Above: One of the last children to receive an inoculation at a free clinic due to a shortage in the vaccine

The fight against Polio

In March 1948 Harry Weaver, the Director of the National Institute for Infant Paralysis, contacted Salk to ask for his help in researching the causes of polio. Up to that time, three strains of polio had been identified but more were suspected. The work would be painstaking, but Salk wanted space and money for his lab so he agreed to undertake it.

As the USA became more aware of the threat of polio, fund-raising for the work increased and in 1952 Salk was ready to begin trials of a vaccine. His first tests were on animals but the first testing of the vaccine on children took place at the D.T. Watson Home for Crippled Children. By 1954, following preliminary results, the vaccine was ready for wider tests.

An end to Polio?

The field trials were huge, involving 1,800,000 children and 20,000 physicians. After the trials, Salk worked tirelessly to process the results and on April 12th 1955 the vaccine was declared a success. Dr Thomas Francis, Salk's former supervisor and monitor of the trials, was the first to announce the success. The celebrations were instant and extensive and Salk became a national hero.

A successful outcome to the trials was so widely expected that fundraising to purchase the vaccine was already well underway and as soon as the trials' success was announced enough money was produced to vaccinate nine million American children. Most of Europe immediately followed suit. Today, Salk's work is thought to have saved millions of lives and prevented disability for many more people. He is regarded as a hero of modern medicine.

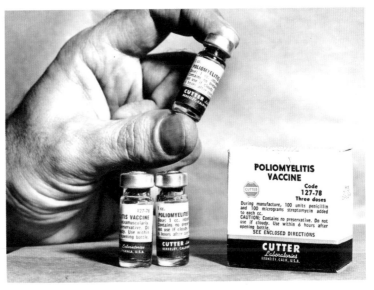

Above: Anti-polio packages were produced by other laboratories to varying degrees of success

1955 Rosa Parks Refuses to Give Up Her Seat

Civil Rights Protest

Segregation

In the USA of the 1940s and 50s racial segregation on public transport was still widely practiced, especially in the South. This was in spite of a Supreme Court ruling that said such segregation was 'unconstitutional'. There had been several attempts by groups working for racial equality to challenge segregation on buses.

One significant attempt was in 1947 when eight white men and eight African Americans made a journey across Virginia, North Carolina, Tennessee and Kentucky. This was called the 'Journey of Reconciliation', although sadly it did not get the chance to live up to its name. Two of the African Americans and two of the white men were arrested. The black men were put on a chain gang for thirty days and the white men for ninety in order to set an example who attempted to challenge the customs of the South.

Rosa Parks

Rosa was born in Alabama on 4th February, 1913 but later moved to Montgomery where she grew up. Her mother Leona was a schoolteacher who actively encouraged Rosa to be involved with the civil rights movement. Rosa joined the NAACP (National Association for the Advancement of Colored People) and became Secretary of the Montgomery chapter. In this capacity she became friends with activists from other organizations and student protest groups, many of whom were influenced by the ideals of peaceful protest advocated by civil rights heroes like Gandhi.

Rosa and other peaceful protesters tried to decide how to make their voices heard without causing civil unrest and bloodshed.

Above: Rosa Parks (centre, in dark coat and hat) rides a bus at the end of the Montgomery bus boycott

Main: Parks (C) riding
on newly integrated bus
following Supreme Court
ruling ending successful
381 day boycott of
segregated buses

Above: Booking photo taken at the time of Rosa Parks' arrest

Rosa refuses to give up her seat

On the 1st December 1955 Rosa was coming home from her work as a tailor at a department store called Montgomery Fair. She took up her seat at the back of the bus in the 'black' section. When the bus became full, the driver asked her to move and let a white person sit, but Rosa refused and was arrested, accused of violating the segregation law and fined.

At this point she decided to use her case as a test case to gain wider publicity for the cause of racial equality. Fellow campaigners Martin Luther King and Ed Nixon, as well as white activists Virginia Durr and her lawyer husband, began distributing leaflets calling for a boycott of the bus company. For 381 days, black people walked or hitched lifts to work rather than travel on buses causing a huge loss of revenue to the bus company.

A victory

During the bus boycott more than 100 people were arrested and more were harassed including Martin Luther King and Ed Nixon who had their houses firebombed, but the protesters kept going. In the end the Supreme Court ruled that the bus company must end segregation, and on 21st December the bus company started running integrated buses. This was a significant victory and one that earned Rosa Parks the name 'mother of the Civil Rights movement'.

The victory came at some personal cost, however, as Parks was sacked from her job and had to move town because of harassment. She and her husband Raymond continued to be active in the civil rights movement for many years to come and lived to see full racial equality in the USA.

Above: Rev. Martin Luther King, director of segregated bus boycott, brimming with enthusiasm as he outlines boycott strategies

1957 The Treaties of Rome

The EU

A third superpower?

As post-war USA boomed and the USSR increased its influence on world affairs, the countries of Europe looked for ways to improve their place on the world stage and also their economic situation. They also wished to find ways of promoting harmony amongst the nations of Europe so that war on the scale of World War Two became less likely.

The USA had seen that trade tariffs and duties had been a major source of friction in Europe after the First World War and possibly a cause of the Second. The US government made free trade a condition of their aid contribution to Europe through the Marshall Plan in order to reduce tensions between the countries. Since US aid was greatly needed in Europe as it tried to rebuild itself, some European countries began to reduce the barriers to trade accordingly.

Diplomatic breakthrough

As early as September 1946, Winston Churchill proposed that the countries of Europe could organize themselves into a 'United States of Europe', and other politicians began to believe in the same bold idea. In 1950, the French Foreign Minister Robert Schuman made a declaration of intent. He believed that the first two countries to form a closer union should be West Germany and France. As the two largest countries, and with a bitter history between them, France and West Germany would pool their coal and steel resources to make more efficient use of them and support industrial growth in both countries. Other countries would also be able to participate.

In April 1951 this agreement was signed as the Treaty of Paris. There were six signatories, West Germany, France, Belgium, The Netherlands, Luxemburg and Italy. The Treaty of Paris paved the way for the more far-reaching Treaty of Rome.

Main: Signature of the Treaty of Rome. On 25th March, 1957, in Capitole, in Rome

Right: From left to right Christian Pineau and Maurice Faure representing France – signature by the 'six' in Rome

Main: Leaders of the European countries, France, West Germany, Italy,
Netherlands, Belgium and Luxembourg gathered to sign the Treaty of Rome

Above: European Economic Community (EEC) has just been created by the Treaty of Rome of 25th March 1957

The Treaty of Rome

Signed on March 25th 1957 by the same six nations as the Treaty of Paris, the Treaty of Rome agreed that the states involved were, 'determined to lay the foundations for an ever closer union between the peoples of Europe.' In practice the Treaty guaranteed the free movement of goods with no import duties around the member states and had the intention of doing the same with labour and services too. It formed the beginnings of economic unity in Europe and was made up of institutions: The European Commission; The European Assembly; The Court of Justice and the Social and Economic Committee. The six states formed the EEC or European Economic Community (sometimes known as the Common Market). Britain, however, was not a member as it was wary of giving up any rights to set its own tariffs. This weakened the EEC and also caused an ongoing rift.

The EU is born

The EEC proved financially successful and greatly increased harmony and stability within the western part of Europe. Britain soon realized its mistake by not joining the EEC and tried to negotiate its membership through the 1960s, only to be continually blocked by Charles de Gaulle who believed the British did not really share a common political philosophy with the rest of Europe. Britain finally joined in 1973.

Today the EEC is the EU or European Union and its powers through the European Parliament govern many aspects of everyday life for all Europeans from housing and employment law, agricultural and health policy. Many European countries even have a common currency, the Euro. Although Churchill's 'United States of Europe' is still not in evidence, Europe is a stable and cooperative community with many common interests.

1957 The Launch of Sputnik

Sputnik

The Space Race

F ollowing the development of missile technology, both the USSR and the USA had declared their intention to launch a man-made satellite into space for the first time. In 1952 the International Council of Scientific Unions identified a forthcoming high point in the cycles of solar activity between July 1957 and December 1958. This would become known as the International Geophysical Year (IGY).

Both the USA and USSR began to plan their satellites for launch during this period. In 1955 the US Naval Research Labouratory proposed a model called Vanguard. The Russians began work on what was to be called 'Sputnik' which in Russian means fellow-traveller.

Sputnik 1

On October 4th 1957 the USSR launched Sputnik I. At just over fifty centimetres in diameter it was about the size of a beach ball and weighed around 83kg. One of the scientists involved in its development, A.A. Blagonravov described it as 'the simplest kind of baby moon.' The satellite orbited the Earth every hour and a half travelling at a height of 560 miles above the Earth's surface at a speed of 18,000mph. It was the first man-made object ever to leave Earth's atmosphere.

For three weeks, Sputnik transmitted radio data to Russian scientists although it stayed in space for three months before falling to Earth. The USA was nervous at the thought that an enemy craft was passing above it seven times a day, but the Russian scientists assured them it was nothing to worry about. US scientists, feeling thwarted in their hopes to be the first in space, resumed work on their own satellite.

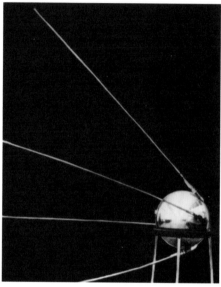

Above: The first official picture of the Russian satellite, shown before it was inserted into the rocket

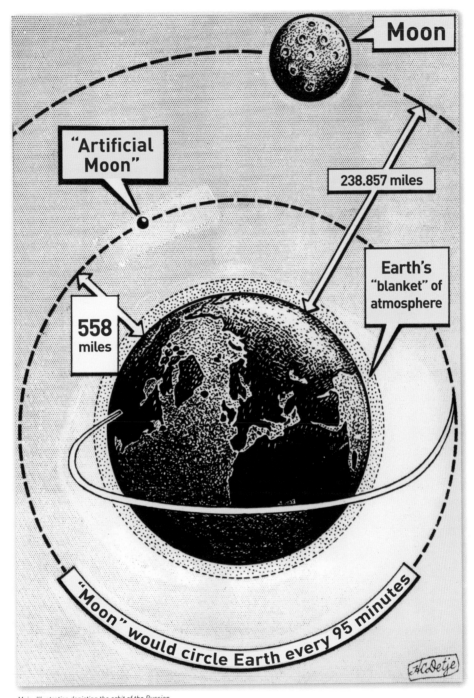

Main: Illustration depicting the orbit of the Russian satellite Sputnik in relation to the path of the moon

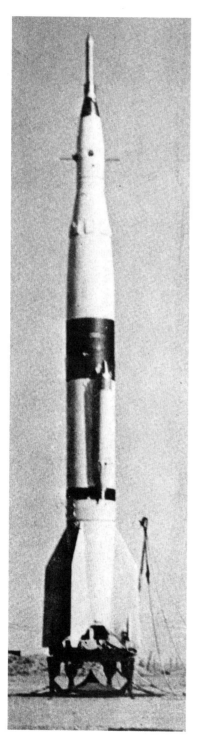

*Above: The R-2A missile that
launched Sputnik into orbit*

Explorer

The launch of Sputnik was the start of the Space Race for
real. The US public was alarmed at the capabilities of Russian
science and afraid of what this might mean for their defence
systems. The US government responded by commissioning a
second satellite programme called Explorer. Then on November
3rd 1957 the USSR struck again. This time, Sputnik II carried a
dog named Laika into space. This was proof that the USSR could
send living things into space, laying the clear foundations for
human space travel.

Meanwhile the Explorer satellite was nearing completion
and following an early setback was successfully launched on
31st January, 1958. Explorer I carried lightweight scientific
instruments and discovered the Van Allen magnetic radiation
belts around the Earth.

The arrival of the space age

On 1st October 1958, NASA (the National Aeronautics and Space Administration), was founded for the continuation of space travel and research. The USSR and the USA were now locked in a high profile and high cost battle of science and bravado to see who could make the next big step forward.

In the wider context of the Cold War, the launch of Sputnik I exacerbated fear in the USA that the USSR could fire missiles into US territory. The USA also felt a loss of face. As the world's most powerful superpower it had been inclined to view the USSR as a 'backward' nation but this latest most shocking invention seemed to prove that this impression was false. The USSR, meanwhile, looked on Sputnik as a demonstration of Soviet power and success. Sputnik was not just a significant scientific moment, it was a significant political moment as well.

Main: A replica of part of the rocket that took Sputnik 1 into space

1960 The Oral Contraceptive Pill is Approved

The Pill

Hard times for women

Whilst some believe that children are a gift and that conception should not be interfered with, many others have looked for ways to control conception. The ability to control conception has been sought mainly because of the practical difficulty and expense of bringing up a large number of children, and also the physical impact on a woman's body of repeated pregnancies.

In the early 20th century women became more keen to lead a life outside the home and away from continual childcare. Women's rights activist Margaret Sanger opened the first birth control centre in Brooklyn around 1920, and went on to meet scientist Gregory Pincus and gynecologist John Rock to discuss the development of a pill that would control conception.

The pill is launched

In 1956 Pincus and Rock carried out trials on women in Haiti and Puerto Rico where there were no laws controlling contraception. In terms of preventing conception the trial was a success, although there may have been some side effects to health. The pill was officially licensed for use by married women only in the US in 1960, and by 1961 was also licensed in the UK. Its popularity grew quickly as women eagerly embraced the freedom that it brought from continual pregnancy or the poverty and difficulty of bringing up a large family.

Controlling pregnancy also meant that women could plan their careers and take a more significant role in the workplace. In more recent years, the pill has been prescribed for all women regardless of status and has been effective as a means of preventing unplanned pregnancy.

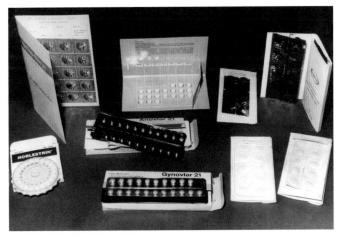

Above: A wide range of oral contraceptive pills became available in the late-1960s

Main: Oral contraceptive pills being manufactured at a factory in High Wycombe, Buckinghamshire, 1965

1960 The First Televised Presidential Debate

Presidential Debate

Choosing a leader

Although presidents and presidential candidates had appeared on news programmes since the invention of the TV, their appearances were carefully planned and controlled. Speeches were written in advance and delivered with little need for spontaneity. This allowed candidates and presidents to carefully control their public image and maintain an air of authority.

In 1960 this would change with the arrival of a new era in politics. For the first time, two presidential candidates squared up to each other on live TV and had to think on their feet in front of an audience. Although the subject matter had been carefully prepared, neither man could predict the exact turn that each debate would take. It would be a gladiatorial contest in wit and intelligence.

Above: The second televised debate between Richard M. Nixon and John F. Kennedy (L)

Main: Nixon and Kennedy (L) share a joke before their first televised debate

The Candidates

Richard Nixon, the 1960 Republican candidate, had been elected in California to the House of Representatives in 1946 and in 1950 was elected to the Senate. He was Dwight Eisenhower's Vice Presidential running mate in 1952. After eight years as Vice President, 1960 was his first attempt to run for President. In the run-up to the televised debates, however, he was seriously ill and lost a great deal of weight which meant that at the first debate in particular he looked pale and tired.

John F. Kennedy was the candidate for the Democrats. Born of a famous political family, he was a torpedo boat commander in World War Two and the Senator for Massachusetts from 1953 until 1960. In the weeks before the debates he had been campaigning in California which had given him a healthy tan.

157

Above: John F. Kennedy speaking from the podium during the first TV debate

The first debate

Going in to the first televised debate on 26th September 1960, Kennedy had a narrow lead. The debate, held at CBS studios in Chicago, was to focus on domestic issues such as the economy, healthcare and crime. Almost 70 million people watched the debate, which is one of the largest percentage television audiences in US history. Both candidates were formal and polite in their delivery, perhaps owing to their awareness of the massive audience and their exposure to it.

Among those who watched the debate, Kennedy was declared the winner but for those who listened on the radio the opinion was more mixed, with Nixon showing a small victory. This may be because Kennedy looked the more impressive and relaxed, whereas Nixon, who perspired and looked unwell, made a poorer visual impression.

Above: Nixon speaking during the first TV debate

The importance of image

The televised debate of 26th September 1960 highlighted that in the age of television the way you looked and the way you presented yourself was just as important as what you said and what you believed. Kennedy went on to win the election and is one of the most celebrated presidents. Nixon also got his chance later when he was finally elected in 1968, a year in which he refused to participate in televised debate.

Televised debates are still a huge event in the US and around the world as candidates use them as a platform for both their opinions and their public appeal. Some would argue that it makes electioneering into too much of a circus but for many it is the best opportunity to see what a politician is really made of and as such aids the causes of democracy and political involvement.

Main: Republican vice
president Richard
Nixon (1913–1994)
(L) and democratic
senator John F.
Kennedy (1917–1963)
take part in a televised
debate during their
presidential campaign

1961–1980

1962 Khruschev Removes Missiles from Cuba

Cuban Crisis

The Bay of Pigs

Tension between the USA and the USSR had steadily mounted throughout the Cold War of the 1950s. One of the major issues was Berlin, where the USSR under President Nikita Khruschev made no secret of its continued desire to occupy West Berlin, surrounded as it was by communist-controlled East Germany.

A particular escalation in tension had occurred, however, in 1959 when the government of Cuba was overturned by the communist Fidel Castro, a friend of Khruschev's. The US government was nervous at having a communist government so close to its borders and on 17th April 1961 ordered an invasion of Cuba by Cuban exiles living in the US at a place called the Bay of Pigs. The invasion, which was meant to overthrow Castro, ended in failure.

Above: CND (Campaign for Nuclear Disarmament) members marching in Oxford Street, London, protesting against the United States' action over the Cuban missile crisis

*Above: US missiles poised ready to launch, during
the military build-up due to the Cuban crisis*

Missiles arrive in Cuba

On 16th October 1962, Kennedy's national security assistant,
McGeorge Bundy, brought photographs to Kennedy's bedroom
in the morning that had been taken by a U2 spy plane flying
over Cuba. In spite of Khrushchev's promises that no nuclear
missiles would be placed in Cuba the photographs clearly
showed a missile base was being built.

Gathering a team of experts, Kennedy began secret talks.
No immediate challenge was made to the Soviets until a plan
had been formulated as it was impossible to know what the
outcome of such a challenge would be. If Khruschev refused to
move the weapons, the US would be left with little option other
than to begin its own nuclear attack, which was something they
were desperate to avoid. Previous calculations about a nuclear
war between the two countries had concluded that the whole
Northern Hemisphere could be effectively wiped out.

Main: Group of women from Women Strike for Peace

Above: Navy Picket Ship, the Vesole, intercepting missile carrying Soviet ship Potzunov

Above: President John F Kennedy making an address on the Cuban Missile Crisis

The world holds its breath

On 22nd October, Kennedy announced to the country the existence of the missiles in Cuba. Simultaneously he ordered a naval blockade or quarantine of Cuba so that no more military supplies could be brought in. The quarantine was also an opportunity to demand the removal of the missiles whilst seeking a diplomatic solution. There was no way to predict what the USSR would do next.

On 26th October Khruschev contacted Kennedy to say that he would withdraw the missiles if Kennedy promised not to invade Cuba. He also demanded the removal of the USA's missiles in Turkey although later he backed down on this point. The brinkmanship of the Cuban Missile crisis was over, and Kennedy had appeared to come out on top.

The Cold War continues

Although the world could breathe more easily the Cold War was far from over. In Berlin, the Russians built the Berlin Wall to prevent East Berliners fleeing to the West. The wall was to stand as a symbol of hostility between East and West for decades although the Soviets attempted no further invasions into West Berlin.

Nuclear war, however, had been avoided owing to the prudence of both leaders, who ultimately realized that once blood had been spilled on either side, the consequences for everyone were too terrible to contemplate. The spectre of nuclear war, however, continues to hang over the world even today. People around the world still imagine the terror and create practical survival plans for use in the case of nuclear war and its aftermath. It may be that this terror is what keeps the reality of war at bay.

Main: Activists holding placards at the March on Washington
for Jobs and Freedom, Washington DC, 28th August 1963

1963 The March on Washington DC

March on Washington

Injustice continues

Despite growing awareness of human rights, including the Universal Declaration of Human Rights, segregation and racial inequality was still the rule in the Deep South of the USA in the early 1960s. Strident civil rights leaders emerged such as Martin Luther King Jr. of the Southern Christian Leadership Conference, and Philip Wilkins of the National Association for the Advancement of Colored People, who spoke out about injustice and increasingly attracted the attention of the government and white America.

In 1963 there was a particular period of racial unrest and civil rights demonstrations. When young black protesters in Birmingham, Alabama, were targeted with fire hoses and attack dogs, the pictures appeared on news programmes and there was a national outcry.

Planning the march

Although most newspapers were opposed to the march on Washington, President Kennedy was in favour. He was, however, afraid that opposition to the March would jeopardize a planned Civil Rights Act.

Bayard Rustin was given overall control of the march and he managed to persuade all the main civil rights groups to attend the planned protest at the Lincoln Memorial. The stated aims of the march were the elimination of racial segregation in schools; protection against police brutality; a major public-works programme to provide jobs; the passage of a law prohibiting racial discrimination in hiring work; a $2 an hour minimum wage and self-government for the District of Columbia, which had a black majority.

Above: American civil rights campaigner Martin Luther King Jnr

Above: King said the march was 'the greatest demonstration of freedom in the history of the United States'

Above: The march and rally provided the setting for the Reverend Martin Luther King Jr's iconic 'I Have a Dream' speech

The day of the march

No one was sure how many people would arrive for the march but on August 28th between 250,000 and 400,000 people arrived to march from the Washington Monument to the Lincoln Memorial. Around a third of marchers were white. There was no trouble or violence at the march which had the character more of a celebration than a protest. Many famous faces were there including Bob Dylan and Joan Baez. Charlton Heston read a speech by James Baldwin representing other actors who supported the civil rights marchers.

Each of the principal civil rights leaders stood up and spoke in rousing terms, challenging the government and the people to bring an end to inequality.

I Have a Dream

Most famously, the March on Washington was where Martin Luther King Jr made his great speech of harmony and reconciliation:

'I say to you today, my friends, so even though we face the difficulties of today and tomorrow, I still have a dream. It is a dream that is deeply rooted in the American dream.

I have a dream that one day this nation will rise up and live out the true meaning of its creed: 'We hold these truths to be self-evident, that all men are created equal.'

I have a dream that on the red hills of Georgia the sons of former slaves and the sons of former slave owners will be able to sit down together at the table of brotherhood.

I have a dream that my four little children will one day live in a nation where they will not be judged by the color of their skin but by the content of their character. I have a dream today.'

1963 The Assassination of President John F. Kennedy

JFK Assassination

A successful presidency

Towards the end of 1963 John F. Kennedy had held the office of President for almost three years. In spite of some difficult times, especially over the Cuban Missile Crisis, Kennedy had steered a steady course and was popular among voters for his support of civil rights and fair taxes. At the start of November he planned to visit some key cities to test out policies and gather support as a start to his second presidential campaign.

A visit to Texas was planned for the 21st and 22nd of November which would take in five cities. Kennedy and his wife Jackie had lost a baby in August and this trip would also be her first extended appearance in public since that devastating loss. On November 21st they visited San Antonio before ending the day at Fort Worth.

November 22nd

The President and his wife had breakfast at the Texas Hotel and Kennedy came out to speak to some supporters who had waited in the rain to see him. After addressing the Fort Worth Chamber of Commerce, to whom Kennedy described the USA as 'the keystone in the arch of freedom,' the President and his wife boarded Air Force One for the short flight to Dallas.

When the plane touched down in Dallas, the Kennedys spent a few moments talking to well-wishers and Jackie was given a bouquet of red roses. Then they got into an open-top car behind Governor John Connally and his wife Nellie. With the Vice President Lyndon Johnson in another car, the destination for the procession was the Trade Mart in downtown Dallas, where the President was due to give a talk. The ten mile route to town was lined with supporters wanting to see their young President and his wife.

Above: Newspaper announcing John F. Kennedy's assassination

Main: Portrait of President
John F. Kennedy, 1963

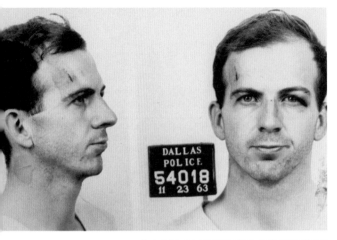

Above: Police mug shot of alleged assassin, Lee Harvey Oswald

Assassination

At about 12.30 the car carrying the President and his wife turned off Main Street at Dealey Plaza. As it was passing the Texas School Book Depository, gunshots rang out across the waiting crowds. The President had been shot in the head and neck. He slumped forward leaving his wife confused and desperate. The car quickly sped towards the nearby Parkland Memorial Hospital but the President could not be saved and was declared dead at 1pm, shortly after last rites had been administered. Governor Connally was also shot in the chest but later made a full recovery.

Within minutes of the shooting, a recent employee of the Book Depository, Lee Harvey Oswald, was arrested for the assassination of the President and also the killing of a police officer immediately afterwards.

A mysterious turn of events

Although he denied wanting to shoot John F. Kennedy and said he was a 'patsy', the evidence against Lee Harvey Oswald was overwhelming. He was, however, never to stand trial. On 24th November as Oswald was being transferred to Dallas county jail he himself was shot by Jack Ruby, a nightclub owner. Ruby was rumored to have connections to the mafia and on this basis many theories have continued to circulate about the possible, secret reasons for the assassination of the President.

Lyndon Johnson was sworn in as President immediately after Kennedy's death. President Kennedy was buried at Arlington Cemetery a few days later and the eyes of the world looked on in sadness as his wife and two small children followed the coffin to its final resting place.

*Main: The presidential motorcade moving through Dallas a
few moments before John F. Kennedy was shot*

Main: John F. Kennedy motorcade, Dallas, Texas USA, 22nd November 1963

1967 The First Human Heart Transplant

Heart Transplant

Early Transplantation

Following the first successful kidney transplantation in 1953, surgeons had undertaken several years of research on animals to see whether a successful heart transplant could be achieved. In the USA the leading figure in this kind of research was Norman Shumway of Stanford Hospital in San Francisco, California. He carried out many heart transplants on dogs in order to research whether successful transplantation in humans could take place.

One of the biggest problems facing pioneers of heart transplant surgery was finding suitable donors and obtaining permission to use their heart for surgery. Another significant problem was that the transplanted heart was often rejected by the recipient.

Christiaan Barnard

Christiaan Barnard was born in Beaufort West, Cape Province, South Africa and went to study medicine at the University of Cape Town Medical School. He then went to work at the Groote Schuur Hospital in Cape Town as a registrar until he completed his Master of Medicine degree in 1953. He obtained his doctorate in the same year.

In 1956 he received a two-year scholarship for postgraduate training in cardiothoracic surgery at the University of Minnesota, USA. During this time he met Norman Shumway, who was at that time engaged in pioneering research into heart transplantation. Upon returning to South Africa in 1958 Barnard was appointed cardiothoracic surgeon at the Groote Schuur Hospital, where he established the hospital's first heart unit. Here, using techniques learned in the USA, Barnard experimented for several years with animal heart transplants.

Above: Doctor Barnard who made the first heart transplant in 1968

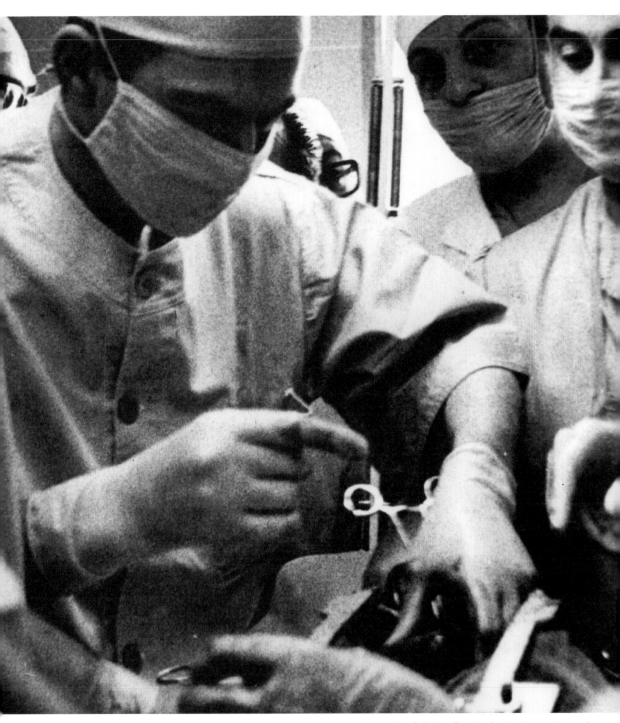

Main: Dr Christiaan Barnard performing a heart transplant on a dog
at La Paz Hospital in Madrid, in order to demonstrate his methods

Main: Dr Christiaan Barnard speaking at the launch of his autobiography 'One Life' in 1970

The first heart transplant

By 1967 several surgical teams including Shumway and Barnard had carried out sufficient research to feel they were ready to carry out a human to human heart transplant. Barnard had a patient, Lewis Washkansky, who was willing to undergo the operation. Washkansky was a grocer who was suffering from diabetes and incurable heart disease. Now Barnard needed a suitable donor and suddenly on the 3rd December one was found. Denise Darvall was a young woman who had been rendered brain dead after being hit by a car in Cape Town. Her father bravely gave permission for her heart to be used in Barnard's surgery.

The operation lasted for nine hours and involved a team of thirty medics, one of whom was Barnard's brother Marius, a surgeon in the same hospital.

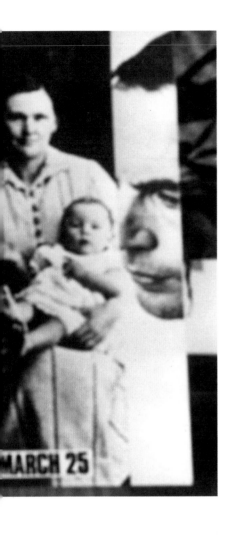

Barnard succeeds, celebrity follows

The transplant was a success as the heart continued to work successfully after transplantation. Sadly the patient died eighteen days after the operation having caught double pneumonia which was the result of taking the necessary immunosuppressive drugs. Other transplants in the USA followed soon after, including Shumway's first attempt in January 1968. Improvements to immunosuppressive drugs greatly improved the survival rate of patients, and Dirk van Zyl, who was operated on by Barnard in 1971, lived for 23 years.

Barnard went on to carry out many other heart transplants, and was loved by his patients many of whom he treated free of charge. He became a global celebrity, known for not only his surgical genius but also his love life, and used his fame as a platform to speak out against apartheid laws.

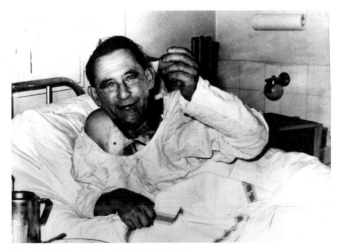

Above: Louis Washkansky, the world's first heart transplant patient, recovering in the Groote Schuur Hospital

1969 Man Lands on the Moon

The Moon Landing

A Challenge for NASA

In 1961 President Kennedy set NASA a challenge: 'We choose to go to the moon in this decade.' It was the latest milestone in the Space Race with the USSR. In the same year as this challenge was made, the USSR made Yuri Gagarin the first man in space. Prior to that in 1959 the USSR had made the first unmanned moon landing when it crashed the Luna 2 spacecraft into the surface of the moon at high speed. Following this, Luna 3 managed to photograph the previously unseen far side of the moon.

The USA felt it had some catching up to do and began pouring money into new technology for space exploration. It launched two probe programmes to carry out unmanned lunar landings and exploration. These were the Pioneer and Ranger programmes.

The Apollo programme

In 1961 Kennedy felt that a truly impressive programme was required to show the US as a world leader in technology. He and Lyndon Johnson selected the Apollo programme – a plan to land men on the moon. Not everyone in the USA was in favour of landing on the moon, however, and some critics wanted the massive funds required by Apollo to be spent at home. Kennedy and Johnson persuaded them by saying that much of the technology could be used in other areas such as missiles and medical research. After Kennedy was assassinated, Johnson continued to champion the cause.

The first manned Apollo missions orbited but did not land on the moon. Apollo 8 was a lunar orbit mission, Apollo 9 stayed in Earth orbit but included and tested all equipment for the eventual lunar landing and Apollo 10 included undocking and redocking of the lunar module. The stage was set for the launch of Apollo 11 on 16th July 1969.

Above: Neil Armstrong poses for a portrait July 1969

Main: The Lunar Module, codenamed Eagle, rises from the moon to
rendezvous and dock with the Command and Service Module

The Eagle has landed

Apollo 11 was launched from Cape Kennedy on the 16th July 1969. The crew were Neil Armstrong, Michael Collins and Buzz Aldrin. After two and a half hours in Earth's orbit, the S-1VB engine was reignited for the escape of Earth gravity. Apollo then began its orbit above the surface of the moon, taking detailed photographs of the lunar surface.

The lunar module, with astronauts Armstrong and Aldrin aboard, was undocked from the command module on July 20th, and landed on the Sea of Tranquility. On July 21st Neil Armstrong stepped from the lunar module to be the first man on the moon. As he did so he uttered his most famous words, 'That's one small step for a man, one giant leap for mankind.'

The ultimate achievement

As well as taking photographs and gathering scientific data, the crew gathered samples taken from the moon's surface. They also set up scientific recording equipment, and Armstrong explored a crater around 60 metres from the landing site. Subsequent landings made use of buggies which could explore a larger area. The three men of the Apollo 11 mission were heroes when they made their safe return on 24th July.

The Apollo programme flew 17 missions in all, finishing in 1972. To some extent the public then lost interest in the space programme and were concerned with other pressing matters at home. The advance in technology, however, was significant and space exploration for scientific purposes still continues, discovering new and greater wonders in the universe with every passing year.

Above: One small step for man...

Main: Harrison H Schmitt, pilot of the lunar module, stands on the lunar surface near the United States flag

Main: American soldiers in a burning village, 1965

Above: American soldiers preparing to leave Vietnam

1973 US Troops Leave Vietnam

Vietnam

A divided Vietnam

For a century, the French had occupied Vietnam as part of their colonial empire. During the 1940s and 50s communist-inspired nationalists began to attack the French, demanding independence. At this time fear of communism around the world and especially in the US was rife, and the US were keen that strategically-positioned Vietnam should not fall to communism for fear that it would spread across the Indian subcontinent. To this end they initially supported the French, and then when the French were defeated the US helped to divide the country into two halves: a northern communist part known as the Democratic Republic of Vietnam, and a Southern, anti-communist republic.

The dividing line, however, was not founded on any kind of cultural divide and many people within Southern Vietnam, especially the National Liberation Front, or Viet Cong as they were known by the US, continued to maintain links with North Vietnam and were opposed to US involvement in their national government.

US troops enter the war

The USA supported and advised the government of South Vietnam, initially under Ngo Dinh Diem until he was assassinated by his own side, and then Nguyen van Thieu. As it became apparent that advice and military materials alone would not save the southern government, the USA sent troops and helicopters in ever greater numbers.

In spite of the USA's superior machinery and military might, the National Liberation Front were experts in guerrilla fighting and were also experienced tacticians. They had the sympathy and support of most villagers and peasants living in South Vietnam and so they were easily sheltered and provisioned. North Vietnam also supplied the National Liberation Front along the Ho Chi Minh trail, a basic, hidden supply route that ran along the border of Vietnam and Cambodia.

*Above: The cover of Life magazine shows a pair of American
soldiers as they carry a wounded comrade to safety*

Above: Army troops running across marshy terrain in Vietnam's delta country

Johnson loses public support

As the war in Vietnam ground on, there were insufficient volunteers to the US army and so the draft was introduced. Protests and riots broke out around Universities and inner cities as people demanded US withdrawal from Vietnam. Most Americans could not understand why young men from their own countries were being taken away to fight in a war so far away. The conflict was also shown widely on television and the US public found it difficult to understand whether their side had any moral high ground in a conflict that was claiming so many innocent lives, especially given the use of controversial tactics such as 'agent orange'.

The war in Vietnam made President Lyndon Johnson's tenure at the White House impossible and he declined to stand for re-election in 1968. His place was taken by Republican Richard Nixon.

US withdraws and counts the cost

Nixon's strategy to bring troops home was known as 'Vietnamazation'. The term implied a gradual withdrawal of US ground troops, covered by heavy air bombardment, while the fighting on the ground transferred to Vietnamese troops. By November of 1972 Henry Kissinger of the US and representatives from the Democratic Republic of Vietnam had reached an agreement for US withdrawal, but the South Vietnamese government did not agree and fought on until their eventual defeat by the Democratic Republic of Vietnam on 30th April 1975.

Above: American soldiers are waiting for the second wave of combat helicopters to come in

Main: British motorists queue
for petrol during the oil crisis

Above: Books such as this were issued by the British government to combat
petrol shortages during the 1973 Oil Crisis

1973 Oil Crisis

Oil Crisis

OPEC

O PEC (Organization of the Petroleum Exporting Countries) was the name given to the cartel of twelve countries responsible for producing and exporting the majority of the world's oil. The cartel was formed in order to resist pressure from major oil companies based in the US, UK and Holland to drive down prices. Around half of the OPEC countries were based in the Middle East.

Tensions in the Middle East regarding Israel had remained strained since the declaration of the State of Israel, especially as Israel began to claim new territory from Palestine. When Israel was attacked on 6th October by Egypt and Syria, the USA immediately sprang to its defence with the offer of weapons and Israel went to nuclear alert. The Arab members of OPEC, angered by the actions of the USA, began an oil embargo, preventing the export of oil to the US entirely, and limiting supply to other countries.

Inflationary pressure

The effect of the crisis was to increase the global price of crude oil from $3 a barrel to $12 a barrel. The OPEC countries also agreed to control the supply of oil in order to maintain a high price. Global inflation had already been a problem owing to the decision by the USA to 'float' the value of the dollar in 1971 and with the added effect of the oil crisis the price of everyday necessities rose rapidly, affecting household budgets and businesses everywhere.

In the long term, the oil crisis encouraged governments to look for other energy sources which made them less dependent on Middle East oil production. It also encouraged greater monetary constraint by governments in order to prevent runaway inflation which added an even greater burden to householders' domestic budgets.

Above: A motorist pours gas into car from jug during 'oil crisis,' Boston, Massachusetts, 1973

1979 Margaret Thatcher is the First Woman Prime Minister

First Woman Prime Minister

In 1979 Margaret Thatcher became the first woman Prime Minister of Great Britain. In doing so she became a trailblazer and an icon for women all over the world. Thatcher's Conservative policies were a controversial mix of downsizing the government and making individuals responsible for their own wellbeing. She believed that state intervention in people's lives should be kept to a minimum.

Born on 13th October 1925 as the daughter of a grocer, Thatcher graduated from Oxford University with a chemistry degree and later studied law. She became involved in politics at the age of 25 and was MP for Finchley at 33, gaining a seat in the shadow cabinet just two years later. She enjoyed a long and devoted marriage to Denis and had two children, Carol and Mark.

The Winter of Discontent

Thatcher's policies were in many ways the result of the 1970s economic crisis. In 1975 Thatcher was elected leader of the Conservative Party, defeating Ted Heath. In doing so she became the first woman leader of a major British political party. At the time, Britain was governed by a Labour Government under James Callaghan. Owing to global events such as the OPEC oil crisis, inflation was high causing a fall in the value of Sterling. When the International Monetary Fund urged Britain to keep inflation under control the Labour Party introduced deep cuts in public spending, especially on education and health.

This led to a period of strikes and public dissatisfaction known as the 'winter of discontent'. In 1979 The Labour Prime Minister James Callaghan was easily defeated by Margaret Thatcher's Conservative Party in the General Election. People felt that the unions and the strikers had too much power and had made their lives too miserable. The British public wanted change.

Above: Margaret Thatcher takes over from Edward Heath as the new leader of the Conservative Party, 1975

Main: The first woman to hold the office of Prime Minister of Great Britain, Margaret Thatcher, at the Tory Party Conference in Blackpool

Main: The funeral cortege carrying the coffin of former British Prime Minister Margaret Thatcher arrives at St Paul's Cathedral on 17th April, 2013 in London, England

Above: The Grand Hotel, Brighton, following the bomb planted by the IRA, 1984

Sweeping economic changes

If change was what the public wanted, that's just what they got. Thatcher's Conservative government embarked on an economic programme called Monetarism. Taxes were slashed so that people had more money in their pockets, but the smaller income for the government led to a period of 'rationalization' or privatization. Thatcher believed the country had become bloated with state-controlled, unprofitable industries such as the coal mines, steel, gas, electrics and utilities, and telecommunications. One by one she sold off these industries to be run as Public Limited Corporations and the public were invited to buy shares.

She also took a hard line with strikers and refused their demands. The most significant confrontation against strikers was with the miners. As pits were closed and jobs lost, striking miners felt savagely mistreated as their way of life and their communities were dismantled.

A controversial figure

Thatcher won three general elections, the second in 1983 after successfully defending the Falkland Islands, and the third in 1987 after keeping Britain out of Europe's Exchange Rate Mechanism. This made her the longest serving Prime Minster in 100 years. Shortly after her third electoral victory, however, she presided over the introduction of the Community Charge or Poll Tax, a system of taxation that many felt was deeply unfair to the poor. Demonstrations followed and people began to feel that Margaret Thatcher was losing touch with her party and the public.

In 1990, following a rebellion within her cabinet, she resigned from office and in 1992 left the House of Commons altogether. When she died in April 2013 her death was accompanied by fierce debate about how she should be remembered: a courageous reformer or a destructive, power-crazed villain. Margaret Thatcher divided opinion throughout her life and even in death.

1975 The Founding of Microsoft

Microsoft

Gates and Allen

In 1975 Bill Gates and Paul G. Allen, boyhood friends from Seattle, converted a computer programming language, BASIC, so that it could be used on an early personal computer. They founded Microsoft shortly afterwards and the company developed other computer programming languages. In 1980 IBM (International Business Machines), asked Microsoft to produce the software for its first personal computer. Microsoft developed an operating system known as MS-DOS, which was released with the first IBM PC in 1981.

From that point on, most manufacturers of PCs licensed MS-DOS as their operating system. Microsoft had got its big break at just the right moment, at the start of the PC boom. Vast revenues poured into Microsoft. Microsoft strengthened its market position still further with the appearance of Windows, a graphical user interface which quickly took off.

Big business

In 1995 Microsoft released Windows 95 which integrated MS-DOS with Windows. It also led the way with office-based software for spreadsheets and word processing. As Microsoft grew so rapidly it was criticized for some practices which violated competition laws, especially after it started to bundle free products such as Explorer with Windows and encouraged internet service providers to distribute it exclusively. In 1999 a judge ordered the breakup of the company after it was found guilty of illegally trying to maintain a monopoly. In 2008 the EU imposed a fine of $1.35 billion for illegally bundling multimedia software with its Windows operating system.

Microsoft, however, has continued to lead the market for PC software and has diversified successfully into other electronic devices such as the Xbox. Bill Gates, co-founder of Microsoft, gave up his role as CEO of Microsoft and turned his attention to philanthropic activity through the Gates Foundation.

Above: Microsoft CEO Steve Ballmer shows the new tablet called Surface during a news conference at Milk Studios on 18th June, 2012 in Los Angeles, California

Main: Bill Gates, chairman of Microsoft

Main: Steve Jobs speaks at the annual PC Forum,
Phoenix, Arizona, 5–8th February, 1984

1976 Apple Inc. is Founded

Apple Inc.

A small beginning

Apple is the brainchild of three founders: Steve Jobs, Steve Wozniak and Ronald Wayne. The company was officially founded on April 1st 1976. Initially the three worked in a garage to produce their first hand built computers, which they showed to the public for the first time at the Homebrew Computer Club. The Homebrew Computer Club was an early group of computing enthusiasts and hackers based in Silicon Valley. The group met to discuss new ideas and is partly responsible for the high-tech culture that sprung up there.

The Apple I went on sale in July 1976, market priced at $666.66. It consisted of a motherboard (with CPU, RAM and textual video chips), and was less advanced than what is today considered a complete personal computer.

A growing market

Wayne sold his share of the company back to Jobs and Wozniak for $800, a decision he probably came to regret as the company rapidly grew. Apple was incorporated in January 1977 and became Apple Computers. Millionaire Mike Markkula provided $250,000 to fund the business. Later the same year the Apple II was launched and was selected as the desktop platform for a spreadsheet programme called VisiCalc which suddenly made Apple one of the major players in the new world of office technology.

In 1984 Apple launched the iconic Macintosh. Its debut was heralded by a movie-style advert based on Orwell's novel 1984. The Apple Macintosh sold well initially, and its sales improved still better after Macintosh introduced desktop publishing and printing software that were especially effective with its intuitive graphical user interface.

Above: Steve Jobs, co-founder of Apple Computer Inc, at the first West Coast Computer Faire, where the Apple II computer was debuted

Troubled times

In the mid-1980s Apple went into a period of decline, perhaps partly due to in-fighting between founder-member Jobs and CEO John Sculley. The board sided with Sculley over control of new research, and Jobs resigned. Apple's first laptop, the Macintosh Portable was launched in 1989, but at 17lb, 'portable' was perhaps a misleading name. The PowerBook, launched the same year, was more successful, but the pricey Apple lost significant market share to Microsoft on personal computers. Around this time Apple started a lawsuit against Microsoft for allegedly copying the graphical user interface, but the case was thrown out of court.

In 1996, new CEO Gil Amelio was attempting to improve Mac OS. After many failed attempts Amelio chose to purchase NeXT and its NeXTSTEP operating system. This was the system developed by Steve Jobs after his resignation, so the purchase brought him back to Apple as an adviser.

A new chapter

On August 15th, 1998 Apple introduced a new all-in-one computer, the iMac. This featured a unique design and cutting edge technology and sold like hot cakes. The new design gave Apple improved brand awareness. The iMac was followed by the iPod, the iPhone and iTunes, and online music store. Apple also opened a string of retails stores, initially in Virginia and California, but later across the world. The stores are notable for the minimal design and open access computers for customers to try before they buy.

Between 2003 and 2006 the price of Apple's stock rose ten-fold. In 2007, Steve Jobs announced that the company would drop 'Computers' from its name and be known simply as Apple Inc. Jobs himself died in October 2011, at which time Apple was the most iconic and successful brand in the world.

Above: iPhone covers bearing the image of the Apple founder, as millions of Chinese users pay tribute to the legendary technology guru

Above: People mourn Apple co-founder Steve Jobs at an Apple store on 6th October, 2011

Main: CEO Steve Jobs holds up the new iPad as he speaks during an Apple Special Event at Yerba Buena Centre for the Arts 27th January, 2010

1978 The First Test Tube Baby is Born ·

Test Tube Baby

Louise Brown

On 25th July 1978 just before midnight, a baby girl called Louise Joy Brown was born at the Oldham and District General Hospital, England. The baby, weighing 5lb 12oz was declared 'quite normal' and the mother was also well. Louise, however, was no ordinary baby but the world's first ever test-tube (IVF) baby. Her birth attracted worldwide media attention and the press hounded her parents for weeks before her birth.

Some scientific and religious groups, especially the Catholic Church, objected to IVF on moral grounds, but following her birth thousands of childless couples have used the IVF process in order to conceive longed-for children and in 2010 one of the pioneers of the process, Robert Edwards, was given a Nobel Prize.

Dr Edwards and Dr Steptoe

Dr Patrick Steptoe, a gynecologist at Oldham General Hospital, and Dr Robert Edwards, a physiologist at Cambridge University, started to look for alternative methods for human conception in 1966. Prior to this, Edwards had managed to produce rabbit embryos by combining an egg and sperm in a test tube. In a Cambridge labouratory in 1968, Edwards combined a human egg and sperm, and six days later, when he looked into the microscope, he realized that he had created a human embryo.

It was quite a long time before a full IVF (In Vitro Fertilization) birth could happen, however, as there were many complications involved in the remainder of the process and for a long time the embryos died in the womb after implantation.

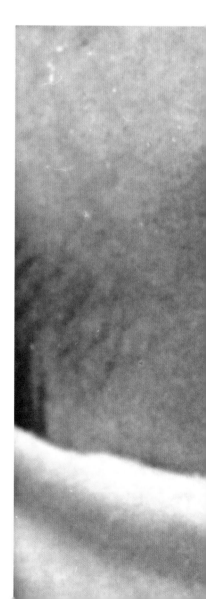

Main: The world's first test tube baby Louise Joy Brown soon after her birth by Caesarian section at Oldham General Hospital, Lancashire, July 1978

*Above: The British public learn through the media
about the birth of the first IVF baby*

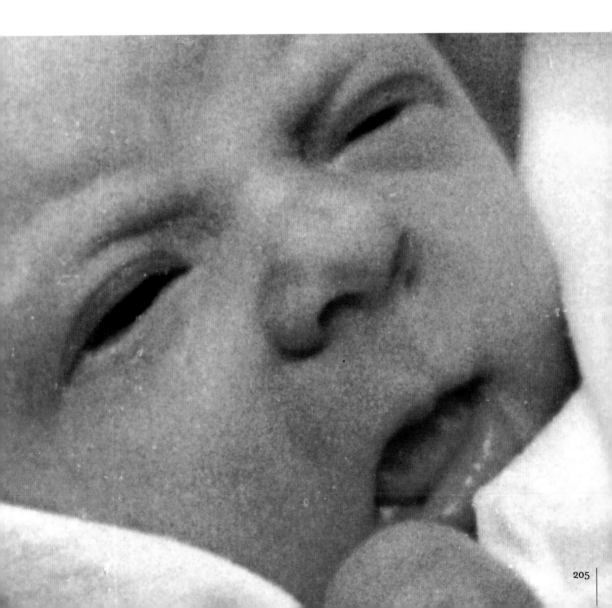

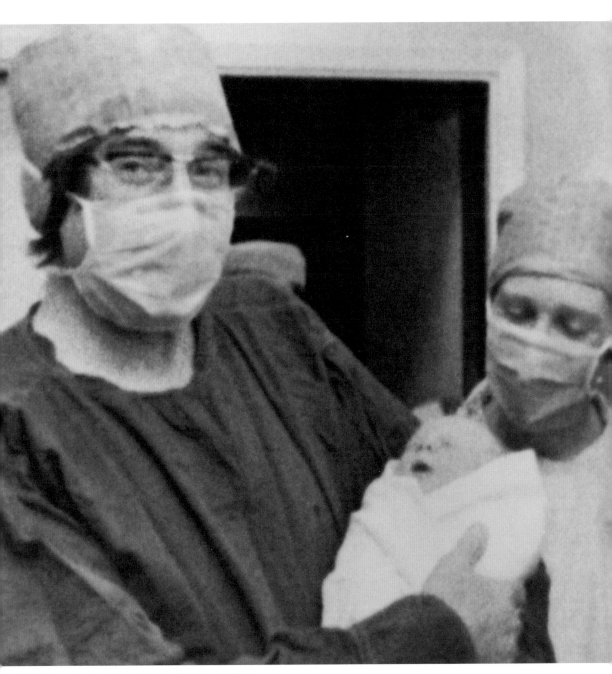

Main: The team who pioneered in-vitro fertilization, (L) Cambridge physiologist
Dr Robert Edwards and (R) gynecologist Mr Patrick Steptoe

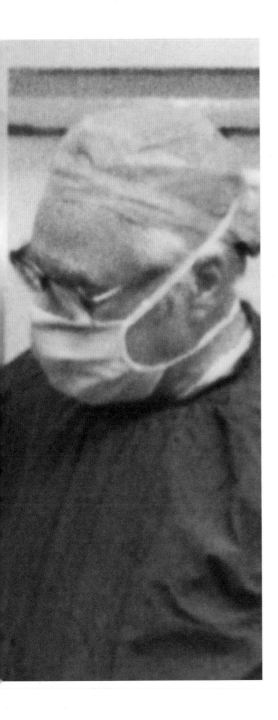

The first couple to receive IVF

By 1978, however, they had improved the process and were ready to proceed. The first couple to receive IVF treatment was Lesley and John Brown. Lesley had been referred to Dr Steptoe after trying for nine years to conceive with no success. Lesley Brown was found to have blocked fallopian tubes, a condition that made conception impossible. Using a long, slender probe called a laparoscope, Dr Steptoe took an egg from Lesley Brown's ovary and handed it to Dr Edwards. Edwards mixed the egg with sperm from John Brown and placed it into a special solution that would nurture the egg.

After two and a half days, the fertilised egg was placed back into Lesley Brown where it grew successfully in the uterus.

The most important thing

Dr Robert Edwards believed that for most people the ability to have a child of their own was the most important thing in life. He himself had five children. The work of Edwards and Steptoe was driven by compassion for women and men who wanted to have children more than anything else, but their work was not without its critics. Many people still believe that tampering with nature in this way is dangerous.

The birth of Louise Brown, however, changed the world. Infertility was no longer a definite barrier to having a child. The first IVF clinic was set up in 1980 in Cambridgeshire and many more have since opened in the UK and abroad. Since the start of IVF, millions of children have been born to grateful couples and have grown up happy and healthy.

Main: Lech Walesa (R) makes an announcement accompanied by Polish Deputy
Premier Mieczyslaw Jagielski after signing the final agreement between the Polish
government and striking workers in the Lenin Shipyard in Gdansk, 31st August 1980

1980 Recognition of Solidarity by the Polish Government

Polish Government

Communist Poland

At the end of World War Two the Soviets drove the Nazis out of Poland. At the Yalta Conference, the Allies met to discuss the rebuilding of Europe and allowed the Soviets under Stalin to impose a pro-communist government in Poland, ignoring the Polish government in exile which was based in London. This was a betrayal of the Polish people. The new communist government lasted two years until it was replaced by the Polish United Workers' Party (also communist). Poland became part of the Soviet sphere of influence in Eastern Europe.

After Stalin's death in 1953 a more liberal group of communists took power under Wladyslaw Gomulka, but Poland continued to experience increasing economic difficulty. In the early 1970s, price increases and a poor standard of living led to waves of strikes by workers.

Solidarity!

Throughout the 1970s workers continued to strike and oppose the government over prices and pay. Then in 1978 a Pole was elected as Pope John Paul II. This formed a rallying point for anti-communist groups in Poland. In August 1980 the trade union 'Solidarity' was formed under Lech Walesa. Its opposition to the government was sufficiently intense that in 1981 President Jaruzelski declared martial law.

However, pressure from the west and reforms in the Soviet Union meant that Jaruzelski had to negotiate with Solidarity, and in 1989 it was allowed to participate in the elections. Solidarity won by a landslide and Walesa succeeded Jaruzelski as President. Poland was the first of many Eastern Bloc countries to peacefully end communist rule.

Below: Members of the Trade Union, Solidarity, who are on strike at the Lenin Shipyard in Gdansk

1981–2000

1983 The First Commercially Available Mobile Phone

Mobile Phone Invention

The first mobile phone call

In April 1973 Martin Cooper became the latest entry into the history of technology, when he made a call on his portable phone. Cooper, the Motorola Vice President, made the call on a cellular phone weighing 2lbs which though technically portable was certainly not pocket-sized. The first call he made was to Bell Laboratories – a rival company that was also trying to build cell phones, so the call must have been somewhat unwelcome.

Prior to this there had been some car phones which used radio technology, but these phones had a base so did not allow the user to walk around. The first cell phones were so expensive that users thought they were just a niche product for the very rich, but since Cooper's first call, the rise and rise of the mobile phone has proved unstoppable.

*Above: Don Johnson as Detective
James 'Sonny' Crockett*

Consumer frenzy

In spite of the cost and cumbersome size, the first cell phone was a hit and waiting lists were in the thousands. By 1984 there were 300,000 users worldwide, although networks were still patchy. In terms of image, the cell phone was definitely regarded as a rich kid's toy and users were sometimes portrayed as image-conscious posers.

It wasn't for almost another ten years that people would be able to send text messages. The first text message was sent on 3rd December 1992 by Neil Papworth, a test engineer for Sema group in the UK. He sent the words 'Merry Christmas' to the phone of his friend Richard Jarvis. Scandinavian company Radiolinja was the first company to offer a person to person SMS network in 1994, and then followed with cross-network functionality in 1995 with rivals Telecom Finland.

Cultural shift

Today, cell phones are used by 87% of the global population and have reached the bottom of the economic pyramid. Their price in relation to income has plummeted and phones are much more multi-functional and efficient to use. Most cell phones now include cameras, movie cameras and access to the internet. Some commentators argue that phones have changed the way we behave towards one another, with fewer face-to-face conversations and more texting.

Network coverage has continually improved and is now almost universal. In Africa and the developing world, the cell phone is now used as a convenient way to pay for goods and services, whilst its services to safety situations and increases in efficiency at work are incalculable.

Above: Chris Brasher talks on a mobile phone during the London marathon, 1985

*Main: Modern-day usage of the cell phone
at the Hammersmith Apollo, London*

1985 Alarm Sounds on Hole in Ozone Layer

Ozone Layer

The Ozone Layer

The Earth is wrapped in a blanket of air called the atmosphere, which has several layers. About 19-30 km above the Earth is a layer of gas called ozone which is situated in the upper stratosphere. Ozone is a form of oxygen that is produced naturally in the atmosphere.

The ozone layer is very important because it helps to protect the Earth from ultra-violet rays given off by the Sun. Too much ultra-violet light harms plants and animals and increases the risk of skin cancer and other health problems in human beings. There is also evidence that bacteria and other microorganisms are affected by ultra-violet rays. Life on Earth could not exist as it does without the protective shield of the ozone layer.

A frightening discovery

In 1985, researchers from the British Antarctic Survey measuring levels of ozone in Antarctica discovered that since the mid-1970s ozone levels above the Halley and Faraday research stations had been steadily dropping when the sun reappeared each spring. Effectively they had found a hole in the ozone layer that appeared for three months each year. By 1987 the hole was roughly the size of the USA and there was also evidence of the ozone layer thinning right around the globe.

Scientists believed that the hole in the ozone layer was caused by CFCs, or chlorofluorocarbons. These chemicals were used for a wide range of purposes including coolants in refrigerators, solvents for cleaning, sanitizers on surgical and sterile equipment and in various kinds of sprays such as hairspray and deodorant.

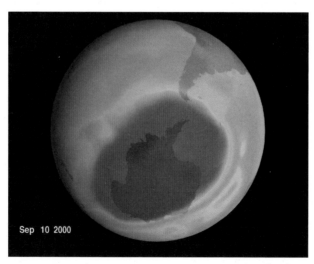

Sep 10 2000

Above: Satellites observed an 11.5 million square-mile hole, a severe thinning of Earth's protective ozone layer

Right: Bondi Beach in Australia, where sunbathers are at greater risk due to the hole in the ozone layer

Main: Members a delegation of the International Youth Organization hold a sign to warn by-passers about the ozone layer near to the entrance of the UN Climate Change Conference, 2008

Main: Smoke pours out of smokestacks connected
to a factory in Taiwan

Fixing the hole

Once released, CFCs from these products float up to the stratosphere where they are caught for 75 to 100 years in the ozone layer. CFCs destroy ozone molecules. Scientists and ecologists were very concerned about the impact of the hole in the ozone layer on global health and well-being.

In 1987, international concern over the effects of CFCs on the ozone layer led to a treaty called the Montreal Protocol calling for a 50% decrease in the use of CFCs by 1999. This was followed by further pressure for a total ban on their use. Scientists are beginning to see a decrease in gases which are harmful to ozone and believe that the hole in the ozone layer is getting smaller, although most agree it will still be there for another fifty years.

Environmental awareness

The discovery of a hole in the ozone layer prompted the first global response to an environmental threat. For many people the discovery of a hole in the ozone layer was the first time that they had been required to modify their personal habits in response to an ecological issue. People used different toiletries and hair products that were 'CFC free' and CFC free refrigerators started to appear on the market.

Since then more 'green' issues have come to light, especially global warming. Lead-free petrol, recycling and conservation have become part of our everyday lives as we attempt to offset the damage done by our massive consumption on the Earth's fragile ecosystem.

Above: NASA pilot Doyle Kumrey sitting in the cockpit in final stages of flight preparation before ER-2 takes off on atmospheric sampling mission over Arctic hole in ozone

1985 Mikhail Gorbachev Elected
General Secretary of the Soviet Union

Soviet Union Election

A thaw in relations

Throughout the 1970s the level of hostility between the USSR (Union of Soviet Socialist Republics) and the USA became less acute, although each side remained suspicious of the other and travel in and out of the Eastern bloc countries was heavily restricted. By the 1980s the economic situation in the USSR was poor after several decades under an isolationist command economy and many people in the USSR received low wages and a poor standard of living.

In 1985 the CPSU (Communist Party of the Soviet Union) invited Mikhail Gorbachev to lead the country. Mikhail Gorbachev brought in a series of reforms intended to make the USSR into a successful, modern state. These were 'glasnost' (political openness), perestroika (restructuring) and uskoreniye (speeding up of economic development). The policy of 'glasnost' meant that Gorbachev met and befriended foreign leaders and encouraged greater economic collaboration with the rest of the world.

The end of the USSR

Western leaders such as Margaret Thatcher from the UK and Ronald Reagan from the USA were happy to meet with Gorbachev. Domestically, however, Gorbachev's policies did not all work in the way that he intended. Greater freedom of the press meant that people in the USSR learned more about the problems and economic difficulties of their own country and their comparatively poor standard of living. They also learned about the crimes of previous leaders such as Stalin. Ordinary people also felt that they had more freedom to protest.

Gorbachev lessened the control of the Communist Party on the Soviet Government. The USSR consisted of Russia and all other countries which it had kept under its communist control behind the iron curtain such as the Baltic republics, Georgia, Armenia, and Azerbaijan. As Party control diminished, these countries began to declare their independence and quickly broke away. The USSR as it was ceased to exist. Mikhail Gorbachev was given the Nobel Peace Prize in 1990.

Above: Mikhail Gorbachev, Russian Politburo member and second in line at the Kremlin, listens during a welcome speech in the Palace of Westminster, UK

Main: President Ronald Reagan (L) standing with Soviet leader Mikhail Gorbachev at Soviet-American summit meeting

1989 The Fall of the Berlin Wall

Berlin Wall

Ideological separation

After World War Two, Berlin was partitioned between the victorious Allies into four zones: a French zone, a British zone, a US zone and a communist zone. The USSR initially tried to win control of the whole city for itself by blockading the other three zones into submission, but was unsuccessful. Throughout the 1950s the USSR strengthened its grip on the satellite states of Eastern Europe that became known as the Eastern Bloc. These were Poland, Czechoslovakia, Yugoslavia, Bulgaria, Ukraine, Belarus, Romania, Moldova, the Baltic Republics of Latvia, Lithuania and Estonia, and East Germany.

The division of Germany into a democratic West Germany and a communist East Germany was a particularly brutal demonstration of communist control as it separated friends and families onto either side of the border.

A symbol of division

Throughout the 1950s West Germany and the rest of Europe began slowly to recover from the war and eventually to prosper. In East Germany, however, recovery was much slower owing to the sluggishness of industry under a command economy and the heavy burden of money and equipment going to the Soviet Union. Many people began to escape over the border and flee to West Berlin. By 1961 2.5 million people had fled East Germany for West Germany. This was a worry to the propaganda machine of the communist party which wanted the world to think that everyone in the USSR and its satellites was happy, and remained there by choice.

On 12th August 1961, almost overnight a wall appeared in Berlin to separate the East from the West. It was the most significant and physical manifestation of the Iron Curtain that separated the ideologies of East and West.

Main: The fall of the
Berlin Wall, 1989

*Main: A man hammers at the wall in Berlin, during the Fall
of the Berlin Wall, 10th November 1989*

Cold War Berlin

Throughout the Cold War, Berlin lived under a strange and alien dividing line and people who had previously been neighbours now lived lives which were totally dissimilar. Spy novels and films proliferated in response to the suspicion and mystery felt by both sides.

The reality of life for people in East Germany was grim. No longer allowed to travel to see relatives, attend theatres or even jobs in West Berlin, quality of life was poor. The only way to cross the wall was either to make a dangerous, even suicidal attempt at crossing it by stealth, or to make a special appointment. The border was only open at checkpoints such as the famous Checkpoint Charlie, situated on Friedrichstrasse.

The wall comes tumbling down

Following changes in the Soviet Union in the late 1980s several satellite countries broke free from communist control and the people of East Germany began to be more openly critical of the government. In an attempt to minimize opposition and confrontation, the East German government declared the border between East and West Germany open on November 9th 1989.

People on both sides couldn't believe that they were together at last. Families separated for decades met and embraced. As the joy of reunification surged not only through Germany but around the world, the crowds tore down the Berlin Wall brick by brick. As the wall had been communism's most potent symbol, its removal was the most stunning sign of a new found freedom.

Above: A German citizen chips away at the wall

Below: An East German border guard offers a flower through a gap in the Berlin Wall on the morning of 10th November 1989

1990 Nelson Mandela Is Released from Prison

Nelson Mandela Freed

Minority rule

The beautiful and abundant country of South Africa had been colonized and fought over by the British and the Dutch throughout the 19th Century, but at the start of the 20th Century the majority of the population were still native Africans living peacefully within their own tribes, although taking little part in the running of the country. In 1948 the white Nationalist Party was elected to govern and things became considerably worse for the non-white population of South Africa.

The new Nationalist government wanted to enforce a policy of apartheid, or separate development. In practice this was a policy of segregation where black, Indian and Jewish people were denied their basic rights and forced to live in a state of deprivation. One organization devoted to protecting the rights of Africans in the face of oppression was the African National Congress (ANC).

Nelson Mandela

Born Rolihlala Mandela and later given the Christian name 'Nelson' by his school teacher, Nelson Mandela was born into the Madiba clan in Mvezo, Transkei on 18th July, 1918. His father was principal counsellor to the King of the Thembu people and at his father's death, the nine year old Nelson was cared for at the Great Place as a ward.

After studying law at Fort Hare University, Mandela went to Johannesburg where he completed his articles in law with a Jewish firm of solicitors called Eidelman and Sidelsky. In 1944 he became increasingly involved in protesting against segregation and joined the ANC where he helped to form the Youth League. Mandela made it clear from the outset, along with other ANC leaders, that he did not want a government that was anti-white, he just wanted fair government for all.

Above: Nelson and Winnie Mandela outside Victor Verster jail, 1990

Main: A jubilant Sowetan holds up a newspaper on 11th February 1990 in Soweto, announcing the release of African National Congress (ANC) leader, Nelson Mandela, at a mass ANC rally

Above: Nelson Mandela revisits his prison cell on Robben Island, where he spent eighteen of his twenty-seven years in prison, 1994

Mandela imprisoned

In the 1950s, apartheid became more severe with protests against the government brutally put down by police. Unarmed protesters were shot or imprisoned. The ANC in turn began to arm itself and protests became increasingly violent. In 1960, police killed 69 unarmed people who were running away from them in what became known as the Sharpeville Massacre. This raised tensions still further. Mandela went abroad to receive military training and to win support among neighbouring countries, but when he returned to South Africa he was arrested and tried for sabotage.

Facing the death penalty, Mandela made a famous speech:

'I have fought against white domination, and I have fought against black domination. I have cherished the idea of a democratic and free society.'

He was sentenced to life imprisonment on 11th June 1964 and sent with fellow human rights protesters to Robben Island, a high security prison where he was forced to carry out hard labour.

A Long Walk to Freedom

Mandela's imprisonment was a rallying point for protesters inside and outside South Africa. He secretly wrote a book, Long Walk to Freedom, whilst in prison to explain his struggle and his philosophy for the future of South Africa. In the 1980s he held secret talks with the South African government which was facing international sanctions and condemnation for its policy of apartheid. After long speculation around the world, on February 10th 1990 Mandela was finally released from prison to international jubilation.

It was a triumph for justice and human rights. On 10th May 1994, Nelson Mandela became South Africa's first truly democratically elected President, where he used the position to unite all South Africans of whatever colour. He and former President F.W. de Klerk, who negotiated his release, were jointly given the Nobel Peace Prize in 1994.

Main: Former U.S. President Bill Clinton (R) poses with former South
African President Nelson Mandela on the eve of his 94th birthday

Main: Nelson Mandela addresses a crowd of residents from the Phola park squatter camp during his tour of townships

1991 The Invention of the World Wide Web

World Wide Web

Above: This computer was used at CERN by British scientist Tim Berners-Lee to devise the World Wide Web

The internet is born

The internet is the name given to the connection that exists between all computers, recognizable to each other via their ISPs (Internet Service Providers) and domain names. The internet came about as the result of the development of smaller, separate networks to serve interest groups, companies and institutions. These smaller networks shared useful information across different locations and hard drives.

In the late 1980s and early 1990s several new services started to develop across the internet. One of these was email, a system now incredibly widespread that enables messages to transfer between computers and other electronic devices. Another service to appear was the World Wide Web.

Tim Berners-Lee

Sir Timothy Berners-Lee, who was born in South-West London on June 8th 1955, is a British computer scientist who is considered to be the inventor of the World Wide Web. In 1980 he was working as a contractor for CERN laboratories in Switzerland, and was constantly frustrated by the difficulties of sharing information with fellow scientists.

He proposed a project based on the concept of hypertext to facilitate sharing and updating information among researchers. He built a prototype system named ENQUIRE which was a mini version of what was to become the World Wide Web. After a period spent working in the UK, Berners-Lee went back to work at CERN in 1994. Here he perfected his ideas and the World Wide Web was created.

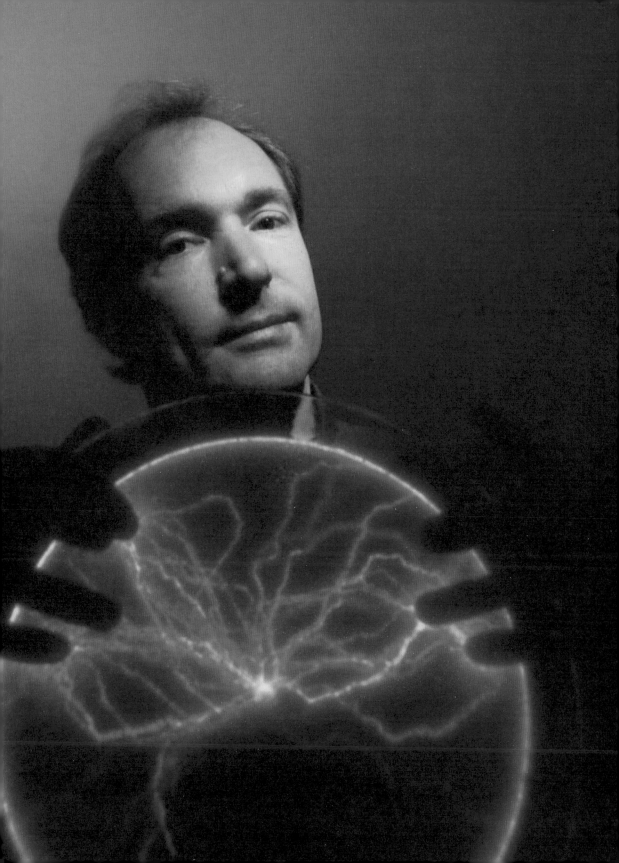

Right: The internet has become part of everyday life for most people

Main: Computer screens showing the internet sites of the search engines Google and Yahoo

The Web

The World Wide Web describes the information and documentation that is placed on the internet for a global audience of computer users. When Tim Berners-Lee invented it he took no payment or royalties for it. He believed it should be something for everyone to use.

In 1989 CERN was the largest internet node in Europe. Berners-Lee developed his 'web' by connecting the internet with hypertext. He said, 'I just had to take the hypertext idea and connect it to the Transmission Control Protocol and domain name system ideas.'

Most of the technology involved in the web had all been designed already. Berners-Lee put them all together by thinking at a higher and more abstract level about how an even greater level of interconnectivity of ideas could be achieved. His work, and his generosity at giving it away for free, was celebrated at the opening ceremony to the London Olympics in 2012.

The Information Age

The World Wide Web has facilitated the transfer and availability of information in a way that could only have been dreamed of even forty years ago. The commercialization of the internet has made terms like 'browsing' and 'search engine' commonplace. New technology has made use of the internet ever easier and developments like Broadband and Wifi have made access to the web quicker and more reliable and enabled a wide variety of new social interaction.

Many have described the web as a source of liberation and opportunity as it allows anyone to express an opinion, publish their work or just show everyone what they look like. As the information age moves on however, the one indisputable fact is that there is no going back: the World Wide Web is here to stay.

1994 Founding of Amazon.com

Amazon

Jeff Bezos

Jeff Bezos was born on 12th January 1964 in Albuquerque, New Mexico. Although descended from a ranch-owning family he showed intense scientific interests from an early age and graduated from Princeton University with a computer science degree. He then had a successful job on Wall Street. Early on in the internet era, however, he spotted the opportunities that existed for selling on the internet and so left his job to start a business.

Bezos set up a site called Amazon which sold books. He asked some friends to test the site before he went live with it and within a month the site had sold books not only all over the USA but in 45 other countries.

Amazon is a phenomenon

Many people expected established book retailers to put Amazon out of business, or at least to create their own successful on-line presence, but something about the ease and user-friendliness of Amazon kept customers coming back. Within two months, sales topped $20,000 a week. The business was expensive to run and didn't turn a full-year profit until 2003, but by 2008 the company's revenue had reached $4 billion.

Part of the company's rapid success can be put down to its innovation in areas like emailing order confirmation, listing best sellers and recommending products bought by other people that have been favourably reviewed. Amazon also started to gather information on its users' preferences so that it could tailor its purchasing suggestions more accurately.

Above: Amazon.com Chief Logistics Officer Jimmy Wright, 1999

Main: Amazon.com Chairman and CEO Jeff Bezos discusses new features of the company's website during a speech at the PC Expo in New York 28th June, 2000

*Above: Jeff Bezos during an interview with host
Jay Leno on 29th December, 1999*

Amazon, the enemy of books?

As Amazon grew internationally many high street booksellers
started to close as people were attracted to the competitive
pricing and ease of shopping online. Some people started
to say that books themselves were in danger as consumers
were denied the opportunity to browse through a bookshop
discovering new authors. Borders book stores all closed,
along with book stores like Ottakars and Dillons in the UK.

Amazon, however, felt that consumers came to them because
they liked the products and customer service that they received
and broadened its product base to include music, films,
electrical products, toys and games and eventually clothes,
jewellery and furniture. In 2007 Amazon produced its own
e-book the Kindle. This was the first portable e-book reader
to become widely popular.

The e-commerce phenomenon

Amazon is the largest company in the e-commerce revolution
and is responsible for many of the features and facilities found
in all e-commerce. For good or bad, online selling has changed
the way people shop. Up until the end of the 1990s shopping
was mainly done on a high street or in a supermarket but now
almost everything can be bought online.

Some people mourn the 'death' of the high street, feeling that
the heart has gone from towns where shops and businesses
have previously flourished. Most people, however, enjoy the
convenience of shopping online and advertisers and retailers
must alter the way they market their goods to a new internet
generation, or face extinction.

Main: Portrait of American businessman and Amazon.com CEO Jeff Bezos poses in an aisle of bookshelves with a shopping cart full of books and compact discs, Seattle, Washington, September 1998

Main: Dolly, the world's first cloned sheep, 1997

1996 The First Cloned Sheep

Dolly the Sheep

A remarkable sheep!

Dolly the sheep, named after country and western singer Dolly Parton, was born on July 5th 1996 at the Roslin Institute near Edinburgh, Scotland. She was, however, no ordinary sheep. Dolly was the first sheep to be successfully cloned and her birth caused a worldwide sensation.

Produced from the cell of another adult sheep, Dolly's embryo was created in a test tube and then implanted into another female sheep in order to be born. When she was born, Dolly grew normally and had no birth defects. She later mated with a welsh mountain ram and had four of her own children. Dolly died in February 2003 of a lung disease common in sheep, but by that time she had proved to be of huge value to scientific research.

How Dolly changed the world

The birth of Dolly was an important breakthrough for genetics. Although all cells in an adult animal have the same genetic code, these become specialized or differentiated as they do a particular job around the body. To create Dolly, scientists had to take a cell that was already differentiated, and use the nucleus to produce stem cells, i.e. an embryo that was not differentiated but could regrow into another complete animal.

This has important implications for stem cell research as it means that not all cells required for research into illnesses have to be taken from embryos, they can be taken from adult tissue. Dolly's birth also allowed scientists to carry out research into the genetic modification of farm animals in order to reduce common illnesses.

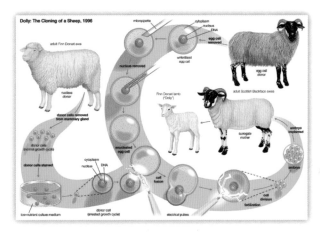

Above: The process through which Dolly, a Female Finn Dorset sheep, became the first successfully cloned mammal in 1996

1997 The Death of Princess Diana

Princess Diana's Death

The making of a Princess

L ady Diana Spencer was born on July 1st 1961. The daughter of Earl Spencer, her childhood home was Park House, in Sandringham, England. Diana's family was well known to the British royal family and saw them regularly on sporting and social occasions. On one such occasion, Diana was introduced to the heir to the throne, Prince Charles. Romance followed with dates and meetings kept secret as the Prince's private life was heavily scrutinized in the newspapers.

Some people questioned the relationship because of the large age difference between the Prince and Diana, but soon the couple were engaged. In 1981 Charles and Diana were married at a spectacular ceremony in St Paul's Cathedral, London. 750 million people from all over the world watched the wedding on television and the streets of London were filled with well-wishers.

A troubled marriage

After her marriage, Diana's good looks and beautiful clothes made her a global fashion icon and the press couldn't get enough of her. On June 21st 1982 Diana had a son, named William, followed by another son, Harry, two years later. Diana was a devoted mother to both of her sons, insisting on taking as full a role in their upbringing as her schedule permitted. She also undertook a great deal of charity work and was especially keen to support children's charities.

The marriage to Charles, however, was not a success and both parties began to have affairs. Charles began a relationship with former girlfriend Camilla Parker Bowles, and Diana had a series of affairs, notably with James Hewitt, and her riding instructor James Gilbey. After a series of public accusations and counter-accusations the couple separated in 1992 and divorced in 1996.

Above: Prince William and Prince Harry with Prince Charles, holding a funeral programme at Westminster Abbey for the funeral of Diana, Princess of Wales

Main: Diana, Princess of Wales in 1990

Main: The Princess of
Wales' coffin is carried
from Westminster
Abbey after the funeral
service, 6th September
1997. The card on the
top is from Princes
William and Harry and
addressed to 'Mummy'

Above: Princess Diana, Princess of Wales, is moved to tears as she cradles a sick child in her arms during her visit to Imran Khan's cancer hospital in Lahore, Pakistan

Death of a princess

In spite of Diana's divorce, the press continued its heated interest in all her affairs and she was linked repeatedly to different men. Whilst remaining a devoted mother, some felt that her behaviour was increasingly desperate and demonstrated inner unhappiness.

In June 1997 she was linked to Dodi Fayed and accepted an invitation from his father, Harrods owner Mohammed Al-Fayed, to holiday in the South of France. On the way home the couple spent the night in Paris. At around 12.20 on 31st August Diana and Dodi left the Ritz hotel to return to a private apartment. They were driven by the hotel's head of security Henri Paul in a black Mercedes. As the couple left the hotel, paparazzi followed them and Paul took increasingly drastic measures to get away. The car crashed into the wall of the Place de l'Alma underpass at an estimated speed of 65mph. Diana, Dodi and Paul were all killed.

A world in mourning

The news of Diana's death caused shock around the world and millions of bouquets were sent to her home and to Buckingham Palace. On the day of the funeral, millions of people lined the route to pay their final respects. The scale of mourning was almost unprecedented. Whilst some saw this outpouring of emotion as hysterical and misguided, others maintained that the death of such a glamorous but somehow tragic figure in such a dreadful way acted as a catalyst for all people to express their inner feelings of sorrow and loss.

As a lasting testament to her work, in 1998 the Ottawa Treaty was signed. This treaty created an international ban on the use of land mines, a cause for which Diana had fought in her final years. It has since saved millions of lives.

Main: Floral tributes and balloons laid in the gardens of Kensington Palace

2000 The Dot-com Bubble Bursts

Dot-com

The information superhighway

In the early 1990s technological development around the world was surging. Communications were changing with digital exchanges, satellite technology and mobile phones. Personal computers and email were becoming more widespread initially only in workplaces, but later in people's homes. Interactive television was the 'next big thing'.

The internet itself was still in its infancy but some could already see its potential both as a working tool and as a means to access new, global markets. Suddenly magazines and newspapers began using phrases like 'information superhighway' to describe the internet and something started to click inside the heads of entrepreneurs and investment capitalists. They started to consider that the internet could be a way to make some big money.

Investment opportunities

As the internet became more widely available, small business entrepreneurs began to see it as a new dimension for any company, whatever its anticipated scale. Organizations like the Chemistry Club were set up to arrange meetings between venture capitalists and visionary entrepreneurs. Venture capitalists were keen to put their money into anything with a '.com', as they became fixated by the thought of businesses that could immediately sell goods and services to the far side of the world from their own spare bedroom or garage.

In the rush to find the best new .com businesses, many venture capitalists and entrepreneurs paid too little attention to an overall business plan, ignoring such matters as profit margin and costs while they were dazzled by the scale of global opportunity.

Main: The mood is sombre on the trading floor of the New York Stock Exchange as the Nasdaq composite index fell below 2,000 for the first time in 27 months and the Dow Jones industrial average plunged more than 400 points

Right: The San Francisco-based pet products company, Pets.com announced on 7th November, 2000 that it was shutting down after failing to secure a financial backer or buyer

Above: Facebook.com is a modern day success of the .com industry

Main: The Nasdaq plummeted following the burst of the .com bubble

The crash

As new .coms were floated on the stock exchange they were frequently overpriced. HSBC carried out analysis estimating an over-valuation of .coms at 40%. Some analysts tried to argue for more realistic pricing but were shouted down by others believing that they had found the holy grail of stock trading. Many .coms were traded on the NASDAQ and it was here that the most significant crash came when the heat eventually left the market and reality struck. The NASDAQ fell from its peak of 5132.52 in March 2000 to 3,649 in April 2000. Investors lost around five trillion dollars, and many young and innovative businesses such as Pets.com went to the wall. Only businesses with strong underlying business plans such as Yahoo and Amazon survived.

The end for .com investment?

In spite of the huge losses suffered by investors the .com bubble certainly has not heralded the end of internet investment or massive global business via the internet. New PLCs such as Google, Facebook and eBay have grown exponentially and have succeeded in attracting investors.

The main effect that is felt today from the .com bubble is that investment has to be sane and less idealistic. The internet as a sales tool is more fully understood and its place in society and culture is more defined, which makes the success or failure of new businesses more possible to predict. Some commentators argue that another bubble is coming in Social Media investment but most agree that the hysterics of the late 1990s are unlikely to be seen again.

2001–Present

2001 9/11

9/11
Attacks

A date that no one will forget

No other event in history is referred to simply by naming the date. That is some measure of how significant and how shocking the events of 9/11 really were. On 11th September 2001 a day in New York City started like every other with people hurrying to work and meeting friends, just going about their business. In the World Trade Centre, one of the city's tallest landmarks, work began as usual.

At 8:46am however, normality was shattered forever when a passenger plane crashed into one of the two towers of the World Trade Centre several storeys above ground level. In the chaos that ensued everyone assumed that this was a terrible accident. Evacuation procedures began although the damage was obviously severe and there were many casualties.

Above: New York City Police Officer salutes at the North pool of the 9/11 Memorial during the tenth anniversary of the attacks

Main: New York City's 'Tribute In Light' to the victims of the 9/11 attacks shines from One World Trade into the sky over Manhattan on 11th September, 2012

Main: Hijacked United Airlines
Flight 175 from Boston
crashes into the south tower
of the World Trade Centre
and explodes at 9:03 a.m.
on 11th September, 2001

2001–Present | Events That Changed The World

No accident

Minutes later, it was clear that the crash was no accident as
another plane slammed into the towers. Panic broke out as
people fled for their lives. Fire crews struggled to evacuate
those that were trapped. In desperation many people jumped
from high windows rather than face certain death by burning.
As the fires took hold, the towers collapsed causing a wave
of dust and debris that spread death and disaster into the
surrounding streets.

As the USA and the world watched and listened in horror,
the news came that the planes that hit the towers had been
hijacked by terrorists and that two more hijacked planes were
still in flight. One was heading to the Pentagon and the other
is thought to have been targeting the United States Capitol or
the White House. America seemed to be under a concerted and
coordinated attack. At first people could only guess where it
was coming from.

A sworn enemy

As shocked newsmen struggled to keep up with events it
emerged that Al Qaeda, a terrorist organization that considered
the USA its enemy, had planned the attack, arranging for
its supporters to train as pilots and putting them onto
scheduled flights.

*Above: A firefighter breaks down after the
World Trade Centre buildings collapsed*

Main: The rubble of the World Trade Centre smoulders
following a terrorist attack of 11th September 2001

2001 The Enron Investigation Begins

Enron

An energy giant

E nron was founded by Kenneth Lay in 1985 as a merger between Houston Natural Gas and Internorth. This merger was formed in order to complete a 37,000 mile gas pipe. From there, Enron grew rapidly, at first into other energy projects and buying other energy companies, but later by diversifying into other businesses such as online trading and risk management. In 1997 Kenneth Lay handed the role of Chief Executive Officer to Jeffrey Skilling, who himself quickly assembled a team of advisers and finance experts. Skilling was keen to satisfy the stock market that the company was performing as well as or better than expected.

In 2000 the State of California suffered an energy crisis and Enron was accused of manipulating the situation to keep its wholesale prices high. Enron's stock began to slide and Skilling resigned.

Malpractice

In 2001 the US Securities and Exchanges Commission began an investigation into Enron's financial activities. They discovered that Skillings and Chief Financial Officer Andrew Fastow, as well as Lay, were guilty of 'creative accounting' on a huge scale. They had repeatedly hidden losses and inflated the value of assets in order to be more appealing to investors. Their auditors Arthur Andersen, one of the largest accountancy firms in the world, were also investigated for their role in the cover-up.

Enron was declared bankrupt with the loss of 4,000 jobs and Arthur Andersen also had to close as the result of bad publicity. As well as the immediate damage to the economy and industry caused by the downfall of two giants it made the public increasingly suspicious of accounting malpractice and new regulation was introduced to ensure that PLCs were more independent of their auditors and more accountable to the law.

Left: Enron is a 2009 play by English Playwright Lucy Prebble based on the Enron Scandal

Main: Jeffrey Skilling, former president and CEO, Enron Corp. is flanked by his attorneys as he walks to the FBI building to surrender

Left: A stranded citizen is rescued from his home in New Orleans, Louisiana after Hurricane Katrina

2005 Hurricane Katrina

Hurricane Katrina

The path of the storm

The USA is frequently visited by hurricanes in the summer months. The worst struck areas are usually well prepared, with homes and businesses built to withstand strong winds. In 2005, however, the Southern States, and in particular the city of New Orleans in Louisiana, were hit by a storm of terrible severity.

It started as a low pressure system to the north of Cuba and moved north and then to the west across Florida, where it caused a power loss to 100,000 homes. The storm continued west, constantly growing in force. Many hoped it would reach a peak before it arrived at the coast again. On August 29th, however, Hurricane Katrina struck New Orleans at the height of its power.

A city on alert

The inhabitants of New Orleans had been warned well in advance that the hurricane was coming. Many left town rather than face the storm in all its fury, but many people remained in the city either to protect their property, to look after those unable to travel or simply because they had nowhere else to go. The world watched the iconic city anxiously as it boarded up windows and braced itself.

At 10am on August 29th, Katrina hit New Orleans with a wind speed of 200 kilometres per hour. It passed directly through the city, destroying lighter buildings and causing substantial damage to others. There was further damage to other areas of Louisiana, Alabama and Mississippi with extensive flooding inland caused by sea surges.

Main: A man wipes his eyes as firefighters try to contain a blaze

Main: A man watches a house burn on Napolean St. as helicopters try to extinguish the fire by dropping water from above in Hurricane Katrina ravaged New Orleans

*Above: Navy helicopters rescue survivors
of Hurricane Katrina from a rooftop in
New Orlean's flooded Ninth Ward*

The levees are breached

Within hours of the storm the levees built to protect New
Orleans from flooding were breached and sea water poured
into the city. The levees had been built to withstand a category
three hurricane, but Katrina, at times a category five hurricane,
quickly overwhelmed them. On August 31st 80% of the
city was underwater. In the resulting damage to gas and
electricity supplies fires started and there were explosions
at power plants.

In the panic, looting began and people struggled to find basic
provisions and adequate sanitation. Similar problems occurred
in surrounding cities such as Mobile, Biloxi and Jackson. By
the time the disaster was over, more than half a million homes
were without power and around 1,800 were dead.

The aftermath

In the days after the hurricane, the army and police faced the
task of evacuating the city. Many people who were stranded
by the storm went to the city's superdome or convention centre
to wait for help but these 'refuges' became overwhelmed.
The roads in and out of New Orleans were almost all damaged.
The Mayor of New Orleans, Mayor Nagin, was criticized by
some for not coordinating the rescue effort well enough, and
President George W Bush also received criticism for the length
of time it took him to visit New Orleans and offer support.

One long term result of Katrina was speculation that if such
devastation had occurred in a more wealthy part of the USA, the
army and emergency services would have been deployed more
quickly and effectively. Some felt the severity of the devastation
was a failure of America's sense of equality.

Spencer DARR is looking
Please Call: 713

*Main: The floor of the Houston Astrodome is
covered by Hurricane Katrina refugees*

2008 President Barack Obama Elected

Presidential Election

Obama's family

Born on 4th August, 1961 in Honolulu, Hawaii, Barack Hussein Obama was born to parents of mixed race and radically different backgrounds. Obama's father, Barack Obama Sr., was born in Nyanza Province, Kenya. He came to Hawaii to study at the University of Hawaii at Manoa and was the first African student to do so. There he met Obama's mother, Ann Dunham who was a white middle-class student from Wichita. The couple married on 2nd February 1961.

After the birth of their son, the couple continued their studies in separate locations. Obama Sr remained at the University of Hawaii before moving on to Harvard for graduate study in economics. He returned to Kenya in 1965 after his wife filed for divorce. Ann studied briefly in Seattle before returning to the University of Hawaii where she remarried an Indonesian called Lolo Soetoro.

Obama's early life

From the age of nine, Obama lived with his grandparents, Stanley and Madelyn Dunham, while attending private school in Hawaii. His mother lived in Indonesia with her second husband but the young Obama wanted to stay in his grandparent's home. He later described some struggles with his identity owing to the lack of a regular connection to his father. He found Hawaii, however, to be a reassuring place to grow up as it was lived in by a broad mix of people from all sorts of backgrounds.

After leaving home, Obama moved to LA, then to Columbia University to study political science. He then spent three successful years working as a community organizer in Chicago before entering the Harvard Law School. On graduating from Harvard, Obama returned to Chicago to practice as a civil rights lawyer where he met his wife Michelle in 1989.

Above: President-elect Barack Obama appears on stage with his wife Michelle following his victory speech

Main: Barack Obama waves to supporters during his election night victory rally at Grant Park on 4th November, 2008 in Chicago, Illinois

Above: U.S. President Barack Obama, left, is sworn in as wife Michelle holds up the same bible used by former President Abraham Lincoln during Obama's inauguration ceremony

Setting out in politics

In 1996 Obama won election as a Democrat to the Illinois State Senate in 1996, where he became Chairman of the Health and Human Services Committee as well as creating education and health policy and championing human rights issues. He was also vocal in his opposition to the war in Iraq. In November 2004, Obama beat Republican Alan Keyes by a huge majority to become Senator of Illinois.

In February 2007 Obama became an overnight global sensation when he announced that he wished to be a candidate for the 2008 Presidential nomination. His principal opponent was Hilary Clinton, who had ambitions to be the first female US President - and still has. On 3rd June, Barack Obama won the nomination and went on to beat Republican John McCain in the main election. On 4th November, 2008 he became the 44th President of the USA. Hilary Clinton became a successful and high profile Secretary of State in his administration.

A President for a changing nation

Obama's victory was greeted with worldwide delight. The arrival of the first black President in the White House seemed to promise a change that many felt the US was ready for after years of fighting in Iraq and Afghanistan. Things, however, were not going to be easy. He began his presidency in the middle of a global recession with high unemployment and significant welfare issues and attempted an ambitious array of welfare reforms, not all of which succeeded.

In 2012 Obama won a second term in office, defeating Republican opponent Mitt Romney. As well as attempting to reform gun law, he also persevered with an international policy of openness and cooperation in an attempt to head off anti-American feeling in some parts of the world. Obama's presidency is of huge significance, not only because he is the first black President but also for his open and inclusive style of dialogue around both domestic and international issues.

Main: Obama supporters from California hoist iconic posters of Barack Obama during the Democratic National Convention 2008

Main: A controlled burn of oil is conducted near the source of the
BP Plc Deepwater Horizon oil spill in the Gulf of Mexico

2010 Deepwater Horizon Oil Spill

Oil Spill

Black water

In April 2010 a huge explosion on the Deepwater Horizon oil rig situated in the Gulf of Mexico killed eleven people and resulted in the pollution of hundreds of miles of coastline. It endangered marine life and had a catastrophic impact on the coastal environment of Louisiana, Mississippi and Alabama.

As the world watched, BP, the company that owned the well tried different ways to stop the leak but owing to the depth of the well it took several weeks to arrange and engineer. Initial attempts involved an enormous containment vessel and mud pumped into the blowout preventer to prevent the oil leaking out. Both of these methods failed and oil continued to flood out.

The clean-up

In July 2010 the flow of oil was finally stopped when the well itself was permanently sealed using a mixture of cement and mud. By this point, however, an estimated 4.9 million barrels of oil had leaked into the sea. Birds, fish and turtles appeared on seashores dead or covered in oil. Political recriminations followed with the White House demanding appropriate penalties from the oil company BP (British Petroleum).

The long term environmental impact was hard to assess but in some areas of the coast sick animals were still being found up to a year later. On a global level it led people once again to consider the impact of all heavy industry on the surrounding environment, and to wonder at what point the cost would outweigh the benefits.

Above: Thick oil from the BP Deepwater Horizon oil spill floats on the surface of the water and coats the marsh wetlands in Bay Jimmy near Port Sulphur, Louisiana

Above: A brown pelican covered with oil from the BP Deepwater Horizon oil spill

2011 Japanese Tsunami

Tsunami

Fault line

The Japanese archipelago is situated close to a large fault line, caused by the Pacific and North American plates thrusting into one another. Earthquakes are a common feature of Japanese life, and buildings, even skyscrapers, are built to withstand strong tremors. Regular drills are also carried out in schools and workplaces to ensure that people are fully aware of evacuation and emergency procedures.

The disaster that struck Japan on 11th March 2011, however, was not caused so much by the earthquake itself as by the resulting tsunami. The scale of the tsunami was much harder to predict and its effects, even on a country as well prepared as Japan, were catastrophic.

The Tohoku earthquake

At 14.46 local time, an earthquake 70 km east of the Oshika Peninsula of Tohoku measuring a magnitude of around nine, tore the Earth's crust in a line about 280 km long. The epicentre of the earthquake was about 30 km underground. It was the most powerful earthquake ever to hit Japan, and the fifth most powerful in over 100 years.

Lasting around six minutes, the earthquake moved Honshu (the main island of Japan), eight feet to the east. The entire Earth shifted on its axis by around four inches, making the day fractionally shorter. People up to 2,000 miles away have reported shaking from the earthquake, and the ground was shaken violently all over Japan. The worst affected area, however, was on the coast near the city of Sendai.

Left: The disaster zone in Kesennuma, Miyagi prefecture, on 18th June, 2011, 100 days after the event

*Main: Tsunami waves hitting the
coast of Minamisoma in Fukushima*

*Above: A house is seen adrift off the coast of
northeastern Japan on 14th March, 2011*

The Tsunami follows

The Japanese meteorological society has in place a system of
seismometers to detect signs of impending earthquakes. As
well as warning about the earthquake, these sensors also gave
warning of a serious tsunami to follow and probably saved a
great many lives. People began to evacuate towns and buildings
or go to refuges. The tsunami, however, hit within an hour of
the earthquake and the wall of water, over ten metres in some
places, travelled up to 10 km inland. Entire towns and villages
were destroyed, cars were swept away and thousands of people
lost in the deluge.

After the first earthquake there were further aftershocks
creating further damage and bringing still more flooding. It was
days before the full scale of the catastrophe was fully known.

After the flood

The severity of the earthquake and the following tsunami
caused damage to one of Japan's nuclear reactors at
Fukushima, were the massive waves poured over seawalls and
destroyed backup power systems. People in the surrounding
area were quickly evacuated but Japan held its breath as there
were three large explosions and a radioactive leak. Although
the nuclear accident was not the most severe ever and the
evacuation saved many casualties, the full effects of the
radiation leakage are still unknown.

Several months after the tsunami, the National Police Agency
confirmed 15,883 deaths, with 2,681 missing. Although Japan
picked up the pieces of industry and started working again with
remarkable speed the human cost will be felt for many years
to come.

*Right: A Self Defence soldier smiles
as he holds a four-month-old baby
who survived the tsunami*

*Right: An elderly woman cries in front of a
destroyed building in the devastated town
of Rikuzentakata in Iwate*

Main: A cruise ship lies on the roof of a two
storey building in Otsuchi, Iwate

**2012 The Diamond Jubilee of
Queen Elizabeth II**

Reign of Queen Elizabeth II

Happy and Glorious

In June 2012, Queen Elizabeth II celebrated her sixtieth year as Queen of the United Kingdom, Northern Ireland and the Commonwealth. The event was marked by spectacular celebrations: a flotilla of boats on the Thames including a beautiful golden barge, a concert outside Buckingham Palace including music from all over the Commonwealth and a church service to give thanks for the Queen and all her work. The Queen and the Duke of Edinburgh also embarked on a tour of the UK to see as many people in the UK as possible and the royal family paid visits all over the Commonwealth on her behalf.

In streets and homes around the UK people came together to take part in events to celebrate the life and reign of a Queen greatly loved and respected by people in her own country and around the world.

Left: Queen Elizabeth II waves from the balcony of Buckingham Palace at the end of a coach procession on the final ceremonial day of the Queens Diamond Jubilee in London on 5th June, 2012

Main: The Red Arrows fly in formation over Buckingham Palace and huge crowds on the Mall to celebrate the Queen's Diamond Jubilee

The young Princess Elizabeth

The hugely successful reign of Queen Elizabeth is perhaps even more remarkable considering she did not expect to become a queen. Born on 21st April, 1926, she was then third in line to the throne. Her father who was second in line to the throne expected to lead a quiet family life in the shadow of his older brother Edward, the heir to the throne. In 1936, however, all that was to change. When King George V died, Edward briefly became King Edward VIII, but gave the throne up later in the year in order to marry Wallis Simpson. Marriage to Wallis Simpson was considered unconstitutional at the time as she was a divorcée.

Edward's sudden abdication thrust the Queen's father into the limelight and he was crowned King George VI in 1937. Princess Elizabeth's quiet family life was suddenly very public.

Above: Huge crowds cheering with Britain's Union flags march down the Mall towards Buckingham Palace

Elizabeth becomes Queen

Although a shy man, King George VI felt a deep sense of duty to the British people, as was seen in his decision to remain at Buckingham Palace with his wife Elizabeth (later the Queen Mother) and family during World War Two and the Blitz. Princess Elizabeth and her sister Margaret grew up to a life in the public gaze but remained close to their parents and shared their sense of public duty. In 1947 Princess Elizabeth married a handsome naval officer called Philip, who became known as the Duke of Edinburgh, and the young couple started a family.

In 1952 when the Princess was touring Kenya, King George VI died. Princess Elizabeth, who had not started life expecting to be Queen, acceded the throne at the age of 26 as a young mother.

The Queen of changing times

On accession, Elizabeth became Queen of the United Kingdom, Northern Ireland and 15 Commonwealth realms. She is also head of the Commonwealth itself, a voluntary association of 54 countries who engage in trade and cultural exchange. Although a Queen she has lived a life of service, supporting uncountable causes and working tirelessly for the common good.

In 2013 a law was passed changing the laws of accession in Britain so that male and female heirs to the throne will be considered equal and no preference will be given, as previously, to male heirs. It is partly just a sign of modern times, but also a fitting tribute to a remarkable woman who has been both an inspiration and a comfort to millions.

Main: Fireworks over Buckingham Palace
mark the end of The Diamond Jubilee
Concert from The Mall on 4th June, 2012

Above: Descent and Landing Engineer Adam Steltzner's reaction after the Curiosity rover successfully landed on Mars

2012 Curiosity Lands on Mars

Mars Landing

The Red Planet

For as long as scientists have known about the planets in our solar system, the planet Mars has exercised a **particular** fascination. This might be partly because of its slightly red appearance, or because it is geologically more like the Earth than any other planets. Writers and film makers have long speculated about 'Martians' or 'little green men'. Others have considered Mars as a possible location for future colonization if the Earth should become overcrowded or polluted.

H.G. Wells' famous story 'The War of the Worlds' written in 1898 created a sensation when it was published. It told the story of aliens from Mars overrunning the Earth and has been influential in forming popular opinions of both alien life and the planet Mars.

The science behind the fiction

Against this background of popular curiosity, scientists from NASA have undertaken a program of research to discover more about Mars with a series of missions to photograph the surface and take rock samples. The latest of these, the Curiosity Rover, is by far the most advanced and wide-ranging.

On 6th August, 2012 at 10.32pm Pacific Time, Curiosity landed on Mars. The operation to guide the 1 ton rover safely to the surface had been fraught with difficulty. On finishing its 104 million mile journey, Curiosity had to slow from 13,000mph to just 2mph before its final descent. The spacecraft then floated to the Mars surface using a 51 foot parachute, transforming itself into a sky crane just before impact.

Main: A self-portrait of the Mars rover Curiosity combines dozens of
exposures taken by the rover's Mars Hand Lens Imager

Above: Curiosity Rover mission team raise their arms at a press conference after the Mars Rover Curiosity successfully landed on the surface of the Red Planet on 5th August, 2012

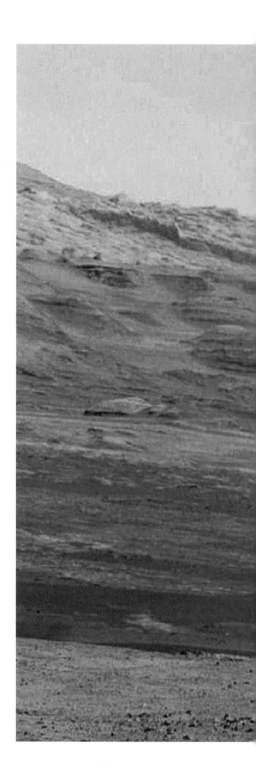

A moving space-laboratory

The $2.5 billion Curiosity has a wealth of equipment on board. As well as a camera extending 7 feet in the air to provide a wider view of the surface, it has four navigation cameras to take a 3D view in all directions. There is also an instrument suite led by a rocket arm which is part rock imager and part chemistry lab. The lab can also heat samples in order to identify organic samples.

Externally, Curiosity has a million-watt laser beam that it can use to shoot at rock formations in order to identify chemicals present in rock formations. It will also use X-rays to analyze minerals.

Curiosity also has a sensor to detect the presence of methane, which, tantalizingly, could signify the possible presence of living organisms.

Journey into the unknown

Curiosity's 92-week mission was deliberately started in the Gale Crater, as this is believed to be more likely than the flat areas of Mars to contain any sign of life. The Rover will explore a 12 mile area incorporating the crater and a mountain, and hopefully the strange areas which appear red in photographs of the surface.

It is expected that Curiosity will not find signs of life, but may give clues to the existence of past life on the surface, and the possibility of future life. Aptly named, the Curiosity project reminds us to keep exploring everything that is unknown in space because one day we may find things more amazing than man has ever dared to dream of.

~2 KM

Main: A view of the lower reaches of Mount Sharp is shown in a cropped image taken with a 34-millimetre Mast Camera on NASA's Curiosity rover

Main: Sky Diver Felix Baumgartner poses with the award
for Laureus World Action Sports person of the year 2013

**2012 Felix Baumgartner Breaks the
Sound Barrier in Space Dive**

Sound Barrier

Daredevil

Felix Baumgartner was born in Salzburg, Austria on
April 20th 1969. As a child he dreamed of skydiving
and made his first jump at the age of 16. He spent
some time in the Austrian military where he practiced
parachute jumping onto small target zones and was part of
the military demonstration and competition team. In 1988 he
began performing skydiving exhibitions for Red Bull, and they
have collaborated on projects ever since.

Baumgartner has made a career out of daring feats that
challenge people's perceptions of what human beings can do.
Most of his stunts involve BASE jumping or flight.

In his personal life, Baumgartner has been connected with
Austrian beauty queen and model Nicole Ottl.

Crazy stunts

Baumgartner has a history of daring stunts including skydiving
and BASE jumping. BASE jumping is an activity where
participants jump from fixed objects and then open a parachute
to break their fall. BASE is an acronym that stands for the place
that competitors can jump from: buildings, antennas, spans
(bridges) and earth (as in cliffs or mountains).

In 1999 Baumgartner set a world record for the highest
parachute jump from a building when he jumped from the
Petronas Towers in Kuala Lumpur, Malaysia. He also set the
record for the lowest BASE jump ever, when he jumped 29
metres from the hand of the statue of Christ the Redeemer in
Rio de Janeiro. On 25th July 2003 he used a carbon fibre wing
to cross the English Channel as a self-styled human glider.

*Above: Felix Baumgartner gives a peace sign
after a successful landing*

Main: Austrian skydiver, Felix Baumgartner, poses for a photo during a ceremony
to get his own Walk of Fame star in Moscow, on 9th November, 2012

Red Bull Stratos

In January 2010 Baumgartner began a project with long term sponsors Red Bull. The project's aim was to attempt the highest sky-dive on record. The stated aim of the Red Bull Stratos mission was to 'transcend human limits'. It brought together experts from aerospace medicine, engineering, pressure suit development and capsule creation.

A helium-filled balloon would carry a capsule containing Baumgartner into the air at 1,000 feet per minute, reaching a height of 120,000 feet in less than three hours. Once in the stratosphere, Baumgartner would launch himself from the capsule head downwards, reaching the speed of sound after about 40 seconds on his descent.

The big jump

The launch was scheduled for October 11th, but was aborted because of poor weather conditions. The mission finally took place on October 14th. High above Roswell, New Mexico, the helium balloon rose to a height of 127, 852 feet at which point Baumgartner jumped. Baumgartner was in free fall for four minutes and nineteen seconds, reaching a speed of 843.6 mph. The event was watched live on the internet all across the world.

The mission set world records for the highest manned balloon ascent, the fastest speed of free fall and also the jump from the highest altitude. Most importantly Red Bull and Baumgartner achieved their aim to challenge human achievement and expectations and Baumgartner became a worldwide superstar.

Above: Felix shows off his tattoo during a press conference that reads "Born To Fly'

2013 Pope Benedict Resigns

The Pope's Resignation

A heavy burden

On 28th February 2013, Pope Benedict XVI officially ended his time in office as Pope. This was a highly unusual and unexpected move, as the last Pope to resign from office did so around 600 years ago. It is expected that a Pope, once elected, will remain in the Catholic Church's most senior and holy position until death. Benedict, however, felt that his health was so poor that he could not carry out his duties as well as he should.

On the day of his announcement lightning struck the Vatican which added to the drama of the day. Devout Catholics reacted with shock at the news of this sudden change, and speculation immediately began about who his replacement in this influential role should be.

To reform or not?

Previous Popes have all been from Europe, the area in which Catholicism as it is today first became established. Many Catholics, however, now live in South America and Africa and there were significant voices within the church, and outside, calling for the new Pope to be from one of these countries for the better representation of the modern Catholic Church. When the conclave of 115 cardinals met to elect the new Pope, a number of names began to surface as possible contenders.

Left: White smoke is seen from the roof of the Sistine Chapel indicating that the College of Cardinals have elected a new Pope on 13th March, 2013

*Main: Pope Benedict XVI on 11th February, 2013
announcing he will resign on 28th February, 2013*

Main: Newly elected Pope Francis I waves to the waiting crowd from the central balcony of St Peter's Basilica on 13th March, 2013

Italian Angelo Scola was the most prominent contender from Europe. As Archbishop of Milan he was known as a religious conservative. Another contender was Marc Ouellet from Canada, a multilingual native French speaker also known as a conservative. Peter Turkson from Ghana, if chosen as Pope, would have been the first black Pope, and was widely favoured owing to the growth of Catholicism in Africa.

The cardinals' decision

The election for the Pope needed two thirds plus one of the cardinals to agree, and their final decision was shown in the traditional way by a release of white smoke above the Sistine Chapel on 12th March. The name of the new Pope was duly announced as Cardinal Jorge Mario Bergoglio, who had previously been Archbishop of Buenos Aires and is a member of the Jesuit order. He chose to be known as Pope Francis.

By this choice the cardinals sent a powerful message to believers in South America, home to 40% of Catholics, that they consider their support vital to the future of the Catholic Church.

Pope Francis

While most Popes choose a traditional name, such as Benedict or Paul, this Pope is the first to choose Francis, which he is said to have chosen to honour St Francis of Assisi. This, combined with his Jesuit background could herald a new era for the Catholic Church. Some feel that there may be a loosening of the grip of conservatism and a modernization of Catholic theology.

The Catholic Church has around 1.2 billion followers, which makes the Pope one of the most significant world leaders. Even a small change in the direction or attitude of the Church would signal a massive change to the daily lives of people across the globe and could usher in a new era in the Christian faith.

Above: Catholics react as white smoke rises from the chimney on the roof of the Sistine Chapel meaning that cardinals elected a new pope

Main: Newly elected Pope Francis I speaks to the waiting crowd from the central balcony of St Peter's Basilica on 13th March, 2013 in Vatican City, Vatican

Index

Picture Credits